Modeling and Simulation
of Complex Systems

Robert Siegfried

Modeling and Simulation of Complex Systems

A Framework for Efficient
Agent-Based Modeling
and Simulation

Robert Siegfried
aditerna GmbH, Riemerling, Germany

Dissertation, Universität der Bundeswehr München, 2014

ISBN 978-3-658-07528-6   ISBN 978-3-658-07529-3 (eBook)
DOI 10.1007/978-3-658-07529-3

The Deutsche Nationalbibliothek lists this publication in the Deutsche Nationalbibliografie;
detailed bibliographic data are available in the Internet at http://dnb.d-nb.de.

Library of Congress Control Number: 2014951364

Springer Vieweg
© Springer Fachmedien Wiesbaden 2014

Printed on acid-free paper

Springer Vieweg is a brand of Springer DE.
Springer DE is part of Springer Science+Business Media.
www.springer-vieweg.de

To Melanie

Abstract

Two current major trends are that todays systems and processes are characterized by an increasing connectivity and that innovations and development take place in increasingly shorter cycles. The increasing connectivity of systems and processes leads to an increasing complexity due to the rapidly increasing number of possible states and interactions. The behavior of such complex systems is not determined by a single component, but results from the interactions of all system components. Typical examples include highly interconnected technical systems as well as social systems.

The development, analysis and evaluation of such complex systems requires more and more the use of modeling and simulation, as it is often impossible to do otherwise. To represent such complex systems, microscopic modeling approaches like agent-based modeling and simulation are often used. Despite widespread use in many application areas, the foundations of agent-based modeling and simulation are much less profound than in other established modeling paradigms. This causes many difficulties: Efficient model development is hampered, verification and validation activities are difficult to perform and evaluation of reusability of model components is hardly possible.

With special emphasis on agent-based modeling and simulation, this thesis aims at two goals. Firstly, improving effectivity and efficiency of model development and secondly, improving effectivity of model execution.

The first contribution of this thesis is the definition of a *General Reference Model for Agent-based Modeling and Simulation (GRAMS)*. This reference model defines the components and structure of agent-based models as well as constraints for the simulation of such models.

The GRAMS reference model provides a framework which guides model developers in creating problem-specific models and increases comparability of agent-based models. As the complexity of systems under investigation increases, collaborative model development and component-based modeling approaches are increasingly important. By providing a common framework, the GRAMS reference model provides a valuable basis towards a common understanding of agent-based modeling and simulation which is the necessary prerequisite for effective and efficient model development.

The second contribution of this thesis addresses the effectivity of model execution. In general, the continuously growing computing power provided by hardware and the portion effectively used by software are diverging. Yet, in order to analyze increasingly complex systems and to execute large-scale agent-based models, the increase in available computing power has to be exploited. The GRAMS reference model distinguishes strictly between a simulation model and a simulation engine executing the model. Following this distinction, firstly various approaches are presented for partitioning agent-based models. Secondly, parallel execution of simulation engines is considered in a multi-level approach taking into account parallel execution on processor-, node- and cluster-level. By strictly distinguishing between simulation model and simulation engine, the GRAMS reference model provides the necessary foundation for executing a simulation model on different simulation engines. This allows each simulation engine to exploit a specific hardware platform when executing a simulation model.

To evaluate and demonstrate the applicability of the GRAMS reference model an example implementation is developed and three case studies are performed. The results and experiences from the case studies show that the GRAMS reference model serves very well as a guideline for developing agent-based simulation models of complex systems. Potential speedup through parallel execution is demonstrated by using a benchmark model.

Zusammenfassung

Zwei aktuelle Trends sind die zunehmende Vernetzung von Systemen und Prozessen sowie die kürzeren Zeitabstände für Innovationen und Entwicklungen. Die zunehmende Vernetzung von Systemen und Prozessen führt aufgrund der rasant wachsenden Anzahl möglicher Zustände und Interaktionen zu einer zunehmenden Komplexität. Das Gesamtverhalten eines solchen komplexen Systems wird nicht durch eine einzelne Komponente bestimmt, sondern ergibt sich erst aus dem Zusammenspiel aller Komponenten des Systems. Typische Beispiele sind u. a. vernetzte technische Systeme ebenso wie soziale Netzwerke.

Die Entwicklung, Analyse und Bewertung derartiger komplexer Systeme erfordert zunehmend den Einsatz von Modellbildung und Simulation. Für die Modellierung derartiger Systeme werden vielfach mikroskopische Modellierungsansätze, wie die agentenbasierte Modellbildung und Simulation, eingesetzt. Trotz weiter Verbreitung in vielfältigen Anwendungsbereichen sind die Grundlagen der agentenbasierten Modellbildung und Simulation verhältnismäßig schwach ausgeprägt im Vergleich zu anderen etablierten Modellierungsparadigmen. Dies behindert eine effiziente Modellentwicklung, erschwert die Verifikation und Validierung derartiger Modelle und verhindert oftmals eine Beurteilung der Wiederverwendbarkeit von Modellkomponenten.

Mit Fokus auf die agentenbasierte Modellbildung und Simulation verfolgt diese Arbeit zwei Ziele: Zum einen die Verbesserung der Effektivität und Effizienz bei der Modellentwicklung, sowie andererseits die Verbesserung der Effektivität bei der Modellausführung.

Der erste Schwerpunkt dieser Arbeit liegt in der Definition eines Referenzmodells, dem *General Reference Model for Agent-based Modeling and Simulation (GRAMS)*, welches agentenbasierte Modelle auf konzeptueller Ebene definiert und eine umfassende Beschreibung der Dy-

namik agentenbasierter Modelle liefert. Das GRAMS-Referenzmodell
stellt ein Rahmenwerk dar, das Modellentwickler bei der Erstellung
problemspezifischer Modelle unterstützt und eine höhere Vergleich-
barkeit von Modellen ermöglicht. Des Weiteren erhöht das GRAMS-
Referenzmodell das gemeinsame Verständnis aller Beteiligten an einem
Modellierungsprojekt. Bedingt durch die zunehmende Komplexität
der abzubildenden Systeme, nimmt die Bedeutung kollaborativer
Modellentwicklung zu. Die Bereitstellung grundlegender Definitio-
nen der agentenbasierten Modellbildung und Simulation durch das
GRAMS-Referenzmodell ist ein Schritt in Richtung eines gemeinsamen
Verständnisses und bildet die Basis für eine effektive und effiziente
Modellentwicklung.

Der zweite Schwerpunkt dieser Arbeit liegt auf einer effektiven Modellausführung. Um zunehmend komplexere Systeme zu analysieren
und umfangreiche Modelle auszuführen, müssen Performancesteige-
rungen auf Hardwareseite, u. a. durch die zunehmende Verbreitung
von Multi-Core-Prozessoren, möglichst optimal ausgenutzt werden.
Hierzu unterscheidet das GRAMS-Referenzmodell zwischen dem Simu-
lationsmodell als solchem und der eigentlichen Simulationsumgebung,
welche das Modell ausführt. Dieser Unterscheidung folgend werden
einerseits verschiedene Ansätze zur Partitionierung des agentenbasierten Modells vorgestellt, ebenso wie andererseits ein ganzheitlicher
Ansatz zur Parallelisierung der Ausführung der Simulationsumgebung.
Ganzheitlich bedeutet hierbei, dass die Parallelisierung auf mehreren
Ebenen (Prozessor, Rechner, Systemverbund) betrachtet wird. Das
GRAMS-Referenzmodell ist hierbei die Grundlage, um agentenbasierte Modelle transparent auf unterschiedlichen Simulationsumgebungen
und unterschiedlichen Hardwareplattformen auszuführen, wobei jede
Simulationsumgebung die zur Verfügung stehende Hardware optimal
ausnutzen kann.

Anhand einer Referenzimplementierung und mehrerer Fallstudien
wird die praktische Anwendbarkeit der entwickelten Lösungsansätze
demonstriert.

Contents

List of Figures

List of Tables

1 Introduction

Simulation is nowadays considered to be the third pillar of science, a peer alongside theory and experimentation [105, p. 12], [55, p. 1], [88], [19, p. 1]. The analysis of many systems, processes and phenomena is often only feasible by developing simulation models and executing them using vast amounts of computing power. Forecasts, decision support and training are further areas that are regularly supported or even made possible by using simulation.

1.1 Motivation

The basic principle of modeling and simulation is illustrated in Figure 1.1. The system under investigation needs to be represented as a model which is suitable for the purpose of the investigation. This model may then be solved by different means (e.g., analytical methods or simulation). The results thus gained are finally analyzed and interpreted with regard to the original system under investigation and the specific question at hand.

Complex systems are usually characterized by large numbers of heterogeneous and interacting components resulting in a non-linear aggregate behavior (i.e., the aggregate behavior is not derivable from the summations of the activities of individual components) [63]. The strive for analyzing and understanding ever more complex systems on one side, and permanently increasing computing power on the other side leads to more and more complex models. Handling this increasing model complexity is not really novel, but more of an all-time challenge. Due to the complexity to be represented within models and increasingly detailed representation of dynamic behavior, simulation is often the only choice for analyzing such models.

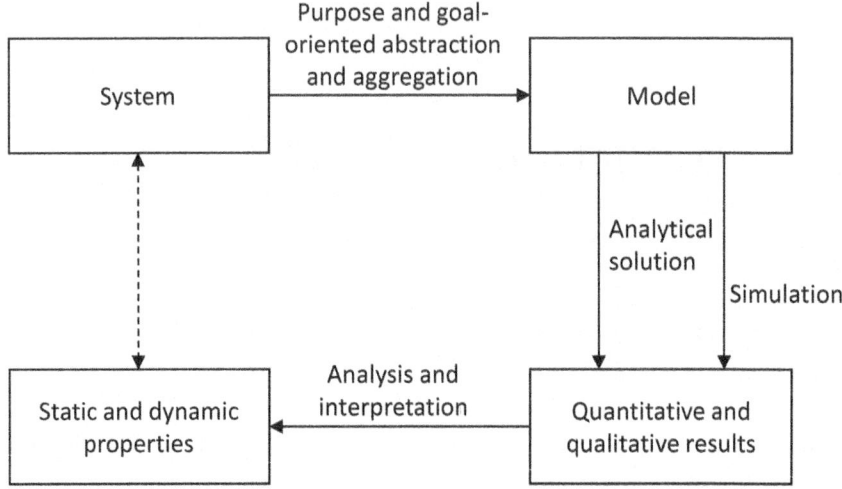

Figure 1.1: Basic principle of modeling and simulation, cp. [140, 13, 16, 74].

Going hand in hand with the rapidly advancing computing power available, a major trend is the shift from macroscopic models to microscopic models. Macroscopic modeling of a complex system focuses on describing the aggregate behavior of a system and usually involves a high degree of abstraction and aggregation. On the contrary, microscopic modeling focusses on characteristics and behavior of individual entities. In this case, the aggregate behavior of a system under investigation is not modeled explicitly, but evolves from the behavior and interactions of the involved entities. The shift to microscopic models was originally driven by domains like social sciences, biology and ecology which are concerned with complex systems composed of many, often heterogeneous, entities [9, 26, 8, 10].

A modeling paradigm widely used for microscopic models is *agent-based modeling*. Due to the close resemblance of the model to the investigated system, agent-based modeling quickly became popular and is often used to investigate emergent phenomena which are observed on the macro-level but result from individual behavior defined on the micro-level [150, p. 5]. Besides in the social sciences, such emergent phenomena are often observed in a business context when analyzing flows, markets, organizations and diffusion processes [22]. Nowadays agent-based models are used in a wide variety of domains, for example in logistics [28], traffic analysis [18], distributed systems [60, p. 278] and various other business applications [93].

Despite this widespread use, the foundations of agent-based modeling are much less profound than other established modeling paradigms like discrete-event simulation. Regarding agent-based modeling and simulation 'there exists neither a unified formal framework for multi-agent models nor a widely accepted methodology for developing multi-agent simulations' [71] [11, 139, 137]. Given this lack, model developers as well as developers of simulation engines have just little guidance and are left with the inherent complexity mostly on their own.

The lack of a solid theoretical foundation of agent-based modeling and the missing engineering approach for model development causes many difficulties. Efficient model development is hampered, verification and validation activities are made difficult and reusability of model components is hardly possible.

1.2 Goals of this thesis

With special focus on agent-based modeling and simulation, this thesis aims at two goals (see Figure 1.2):

1. Improving the effectivity and efficiency of model development.

2. Improving the effectivity of model execution.

The following sections provide detailed descriptions of these two goals.

Effective and efficient model development

Model development often involves the participation of many – possibly geographically distributed – parties, for instance domain experts, model developers, software engineers and analysts [12]. Each party has

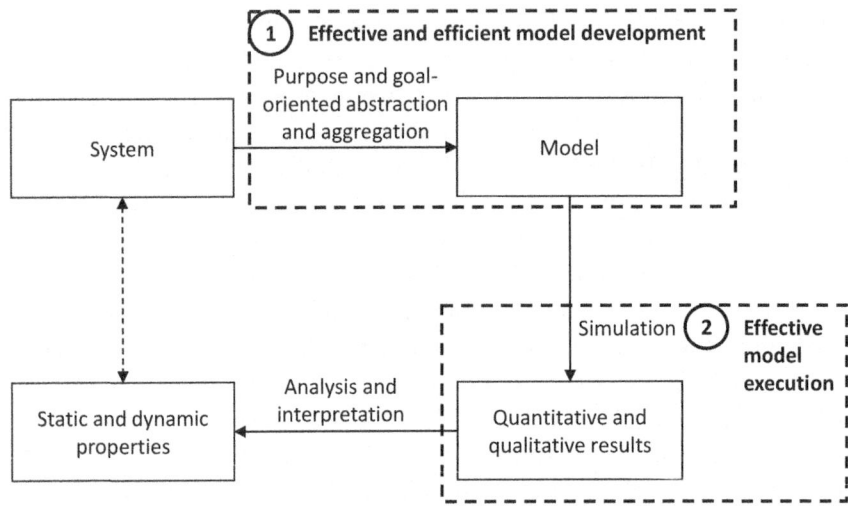

Figure 1.2: The goals of this thesis are to improve effectivity and efficiency of model development and model execution.

a very unique view on the problem at hand and contributes to specific parts of a model. A major challenge in developing complex models is to properly decompose a model into submodels while at the same time maintaining overall consistency and ensuring compatibility of submodels. To ensure successful model development (i. e., consistent development of model components or submodels) all parties have to follow a common model development process within a common methodological framework.

An absolutely necessary prerequisite for effective collaborative model development is a shared domain understanding of all parties – ideally based upon a sound theoretical foundation. Besides a common understanding of the model development process, all parties need a common understanding of the model to be developed. They need to know how a model is decomposed into submodels, how interactions between these are defined and how the overall model is finally executed.

The above issues are related to developing simulation models and improving collaboration between model developers. In addition, collaboration between model developers and developers involved in providing the necessary development and runtime infrastructure has to be considered. In the simplest case, the infrastructure consists only of the software required for executing a model. Issues like providing high-performance computing capabilities and distributed (grid-like) execution have to be covered for effectively simulating large-scale models.

Effective model execution

The shift towards microscopic modeling is closely connected with the availability of the required computing power. While the increase in computing power follows Moore's Law for more than fourty years, software development does not nearly keep pace. The computing power provided by hardware and the portion effectively used by software are diverging. This is known as *efficiency and programmability gap*, and exactly this gap is becoming one of the major issues in software development nowadays [31, p. 7], [87], [3, p. 7f.]. This trend is even accelerated and amplified by the development of multi-core processors which will by far dominate future processor designs [37, 126, 64, 2].

The challenge of bridging this gap obviously applies similarly to simulation. Given the demand of more and more complex models, it is necessary to exploit the computing power of multi-core processors in an optimal fashion [22, 26]. On a conceptual level, agent-based modeling seems to be a very promising approach to do so. As all agents act in parallel, this should allow for a high degree of parallelization. Furthermore, agent-based models offer a high scalability both in number of agents and level of detail within single agents. Yet besides missing foundations in the area of agent-based modeling in general, concepts and procedures as well as actual technical solutions for exploiting model-inherent parallelism are also missing. Last but not least, considering large-scale models and their collaborative development, it should be possible to develop and test models locally while executing them on high-performance computers afterwards [125].

1.3 Approach of this thesis and outline

The following approach is taken in this thesis to address the outlined goals:

1. Providing a solid foundation of agent-based modeling and simulation:
   The solid foundation is provided in this thesis by definition of the *General Reference Model for Agent-based Modeling and Simulation (GRAMS)*. In a domain-independent way, the GRAMS reference model defines on a conceptual level the basic building blocks of agent-based models and their relations. Based upon this, constraints for the simulation of such a model are defined. Such a clear and common understanding is the prerequisite for effective model development (and subsequently for mastering the shift to micro-modeling and enabling effective collaborative development).

   Following well-established patterns, the GRAMS reference model distinguishes between a simulation model and a simulation engine executing a model (within the defined constraints). Although seemingly obvious, many agent-based simulation studies often intermingle these aspects. The clear distinction makes it possible to develop and use different simulation engines executing the same model and producing identical results.

2. Enabling small-scale development and smooth transition to large-scale models:
   Based on the GRAMS reference model, this thesis discusses various possibilities of executing the simulation of agent-based models in a parallel and distributed fashion. The objective is to develop a model just once, and to enable its execution by different simulation engines producing identical results. Therefore, different types of simulation engines are described, including single-threaded simulation engines and a multi-threaded simulation engine. The multi-threaded simulation engine basically serves two purposes: Firstly, to evaluate different strategies for parallelizing execution of an agent-based simulation and measuring achieveable performance

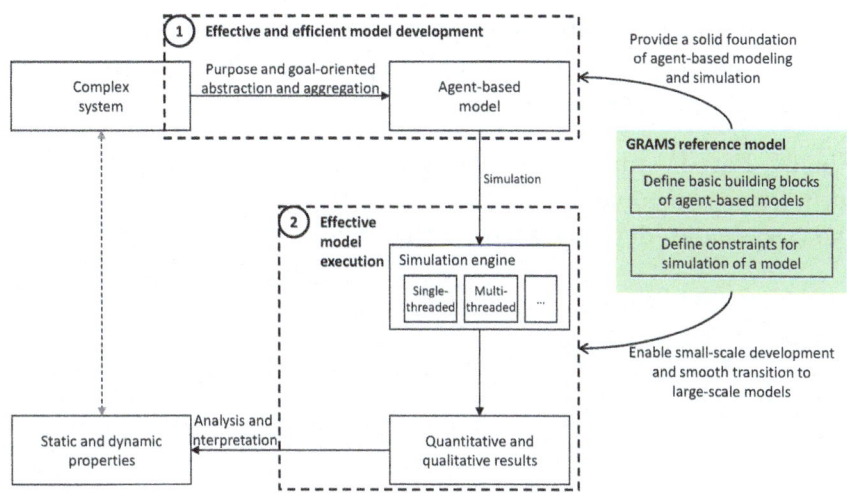

Figure 1.3: Approach of this thesis for improving the effectivity and efficiency of model development and model execution.

speedups. Secondly, to demonstrate how model development and infrastructure development can be separated, enabling each party to utilize its full potential and reducing the efficiency gap.

Figure 1.3 illustrates the approach taken in this thesis.

For evaluation and demonstration of the applicability of the GRAMS reference model three case studies are presented. A further model built upon the GRAMS reference model is included for benchmarking reasons.

In Part I of this thesis preliminaries of agent-based modeling and simulation are introduced as well as related work (Chapter 2). The current state of art in parallelizing the execution of an agent-based model is discussed in Chapter 3. Following the goals and the chosen approach, the major findings are arranged in two main parts:

- Part II specifies the requirements on the reference model (Chapter 5), defines the GRAMS reference model (Chapter 6), and concludes with a brief summary (Chapter 7).

- Part III presents strategies for model partitioning and parallel execution (Chapter 8), and the example implementation and performance benchmarks (Chapter 9).

Finally, Part IV summarizes the results and provides an outlook on future research topics. Part V contains the detailed descriptions of the case studies developed within this thesis.

Part I

Preliminaries and related work

2 Agent-based modeling and simulation

This chapter presents basic terminology used in context of modeling and simulation in general, as well as in the area of agent-based modeling and simulation in particular. Within the remainder of this thesis the terms are used according to the definitions and explanations given here. After presenting basic terminology, this chapter discusses related work.

2.1 Basic terminology

The basic terms *(complex) system*, *modeling* and *simulation* are often used together and indeed, they are deeply connected. Nevertheless, it is important to distinguish these terms clearly in order to avoid misunderstandings.

2.1.1 Complex system

Complex systems are usually understood as systems consisting of a large number of heterogeneous, interacting components [93, 63]. The root causes of complexity are manifold and although more complexity metrics may be found, these are a few typical characteristics often attributed to complex systems:

- State space complexity (number of possible system states, number and value range of model parameters)

- Structural complexity (relationships and dependencies of system components)

- Behavioral and algorithmic complexity (intricate behavior and interaction patterns of system components)

- Temporal complexity (time- and state-dependent behavior of system components)

A key property of complex systems is that no single component controls the system behavior. Instead, the system behavior results from multiple and manifold interactions between the components. The term *emergence* refers to the fact that the system's overall behavior is not obviously derivable from the behavior of its constituting components. Interactions between the components have to be taken into account as well as effects of non-linearity [63].

2.1.2 Model

For this thesis a definition of a model is adopted which is not restricted to a specific domain:

Definition 1 (Model) A *model* is an idealized, simplifying and with respect to certain aspects similar representation of an item, system or some other part of the world. The purpose of the model is to allow a better study of specific properties than using the original system [54, p. 103]. □

In other words, a model is a goal-oriented description of a system that abstracts some parts of the original system with the intention to provide an easier explanation or analysis of the original system (cp. [16, p. 12]). Figure 1.1 illustrates this relation between the original system (i. e., the system under investigation) and the model as an idealized and simplified representation of that system. Depending on the purpose very different types of models are suitable to represent the original system. Once a model is developed, it may be explored or analyzed using different techniques, ranging from purely mathematical solutions to computer simulations. Depending on the chosen technique to solve a model, more specific terms are common, e. g., *simulation model* for a model which is solved by using simulation techniques.

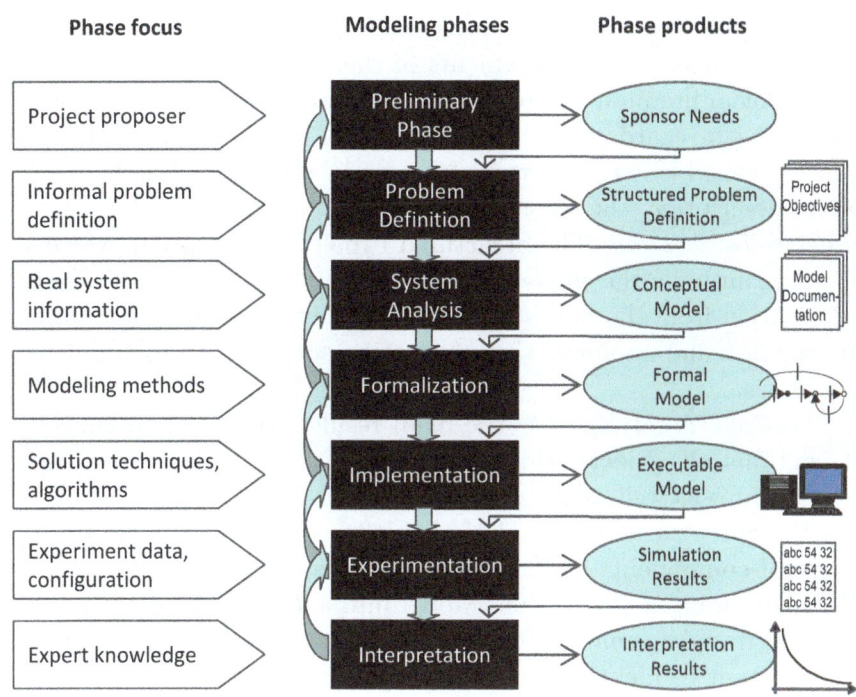

Figure 2.1: Generic model development process [77].

With regard to computer simulations, the results thus gained are generally of quantitative nature. However, the interpretation of simulation results with respect to the original system to answer the given questions may be quantitative or qualitative.

2.1.3 Model development process

In order to be precise, the term *model* has to be refined and augmented with additional information. In general, *the* model does not exist, but rather a model always exists in different stages. These different stages may best be explained following a generic model development process.

In [77, 106] a model development process is proposed that consists of seven phases (see Figure 2.1). The *Sponsor Needs* mark the beginning of each model development process. They document the original demand and requirements of the sponsor and describe the real problem in mind. Therefore, the Sponsor Needs are usually very specific with regards to the actual question in mind, but often miss information which are important for a model developer. Based on this initial description, the second phase focuses on creating a *Structured Problem Description*. The Structured Problem Description, which is created jointly by the sponsor and the model developers, takes up the information from the Sponsor Needs, augments them with additional information and organizes the information according to standardized templates.

The *Conceptual Model* is the main result of the system analysis. It contains all objects which are part of the model, defines their relationships as well as the properties and the behavior of all objects. Furthermore, the Conceptual Model defines the model structure (in terms of components and submodels). Formalization is the process of transforming a Conceptual Model into a *Formal Model* which is a detailed and formalized description of a model. At this point it is important to mention that if the Conceptual Model contains too few or too much information, the model developer has to iterate and extend or adapt the Conceptual Model first. This principle is also valid for the next phase: The *Executable Model* is a consistent and complete implementation of a Formal Model. Differences between a Formal Model and its corresponding Executable Model are nevertheless possible and sometimes unavoidable.

The Executable Model is finally used for experimentation and generates *Simulation Results*. These Simulation Results are usually unprocessed data (e. g., arrival times, object counters, etc.) gathered during simulation execution. In the final phase of the model development process the Simulation Results are interpreted by analysts and subject matter experts, thus creating the *Interpretation Results*. Ideally, these Interpretation Results answer the questions originally specified by the sponsor at the beginning of the whole process in the Sponsor Needs.

As already mentioned, there is no such thing as *the one* model. Instead, each simulation model exists in at least three stages (conceptual model, formal model, executable model). In colloquial speech the term *model* is often used synonymously with *executable model* and one has to be aware of the subtle differences.

2.1.4 Simulation

The term *simulation* is frequently used with two slightly different meanings. The first interpretation of simulation refers to the methodology of using simulation techniques for solving a specific problem. This covers the whole process of analyzing the problem, developing a simulation model (consisting of a conceptual model, formal model, and executable model), executing experiments and interpreting the results (see Figure 2.1).

The second interpretation refers to simulation as the act of actually executing an executable simulation model. Therefore, a simulation takes an executable model (and data) as input and applies a number of computational steps to transform a model from an initial state into a final state.

In the following, the term *simulation* refers to the second interpretation:

Definition 2 (Simulation) The term *simulation* refers to the execution of a specific executable simulation model. □

Although it is possible to simulate manually, almost always an appropriate simulation engine is used.

Definition 3 (Simulation engine) A *simulation engine* is a software application that executes the simulation of a model. □

A simulation engine may internally use any kind of data structures and execution control as long as the simulation is executed correctly. Within this thesis, the term *simulation engine* refers to a piece of software and not to the execution control mechanism or any other

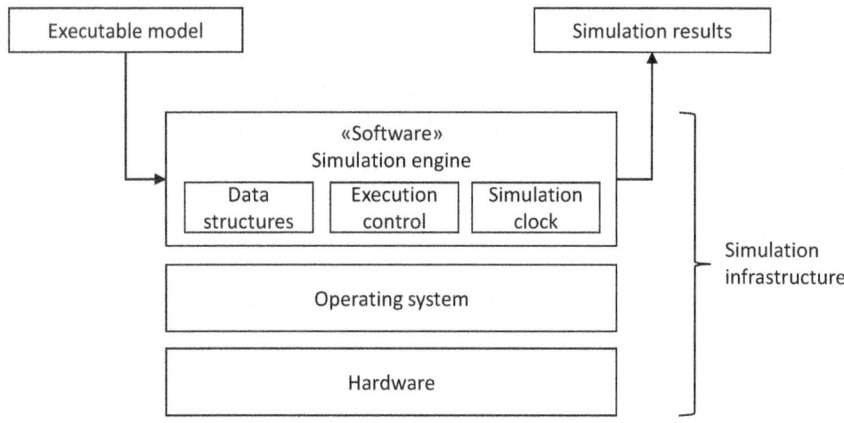

Figure 2.2: Components of a simulation infrastructure.

internal algorithm. The simulation engine together with necessary computing hardware and operating system is referred to as simulation infrastructure:

Definition 4 (Simulation infrastructure) The term *simulation infrastructure* refers to the entirety of hardware and software (operating system as well as simulation engine) necessary to execute a simulation model.   □

Figure 2.2 ilustrates the components of a simulation infrastructure.

Using an analogy from a different area of computer science, the terms simulation and simulation engine may be explained as follows: Given an unsorted list, it may exactly be defined what is understood by *sorting* this list. However, sorting may be done by any sort algorithm, like bubblesort or quicksort. No matter which sort algorithm is used after its execution the list is sorted. Similarly, a simulation may be executed by different simulation engines. The important point is that the result is the same no matter which simulation engine is used, i. e., identical simulation results are produced.

Strictly separating the definition of the term *simulation* and the simulation engine as the actual software executing the simulation provides numerous benefits [151, p. 29]:

- Algorithms for executing a simulation as well as simulation engines may be specified and their correctness established rigorously.

- The same simulation model may be executed by different simulation engines, thus opening the way for portability and interoperability at a high level of abstraction.

- Different simulation engines may utilize the underlying computer hardware in an optimal way. Most notably, a simulation engine might parallelize the execution of a model.

Specific application areas of simulation may impose additional requirements on a simulation model or simulation engine (e. g., regarding update rate).

2.2 Agent-based modeling and simulation

2.2.1 Agent

Agent-based modeling and simulation is a paradigm which gains more and more attention for analyzing complex systems and becomes more and more widespread over the last years. While some authors claim that agent-based simulation seems to be a relatively new idea for the simulation community [109], others argue that agent-based modeling and simulation 'should not be seen as a completely new and original simulation paradigm' [27]. As the notion of an *agent* is the central idea upon which agent-based modeling is built, it is important to have a clear understanding of what is meant by this term. Surprisingly, there is no general agreement on a precise definition of the term *agent*.

Besides the ongoing debate and controversy, definitions tend to agree on more points than they disagree [148, p. 28], [83, 109, 80, 61]. For the purpose of this thesis, an agent is defined as follows:

Definition 5 (Agent) An *agent* is an entity that is *situated* in some *environment*, and that is capable of *autonomous action* in this environment in order to meet its *objectives*.   □

This definition is very close to [148, p. 29] and conforms with the definitions given in [60, p. 280], [59, p. 83], [46], [61, 112] and [68]. In good accordance with this definition, the following characteristics of agents are generally agreed on [108, 83, 61, 112]:

- Agents are identifiable, discrete (and usually heterogeneous) individuals [93, p. 214].

- Agents are space-aware, i.e., they are situated in some kind of environment [83, 23, 120].

- Agents are capable of autonomous action and independent decisions. In this sense, agents are actively acting rather than purely passive objects [148, p. 28ff.], [93, p. 214], [68].

- In order to act within the environment and pursue their goals, agents are capable of perceiving their environment and acting within this environment [68], [148, p. 32].

Besides these generally agreed characteristics, many more definitions (partially very specific to certain domains) exist. Also, many more characteristics for describing an agent are available. Of these, at least one characteristic is worth mentioning. The *ability to learn* is part of many definitions of an agent and refers to the capability of an agent to adapt (and possibly improve) its behavior [93, p. 214]. The aspect of agents showing some kind of adaptive behavior or learning is not part of the definition of an agent used within this thesis. This is due to the fact that this requirement can not be applied to all kinds of agents (albeit to a huge number) and therefore is to restraining.

Definition 6 (Agent-based model) An *agent-based model* is a simulation model that employs the idea of multiple agents situated and acting in a common environment as central modeling paradigm.□

An agent-based model usually contains different types of agents which represent different individuals from the system under investigation. Multiple, distinguishable instances of each type of agent may be present in the model. This definition of an agent-based model does not answer the question whether agent-based modeling and simulation is something new or not, it rather stresses that 'agent-based modeling is a mindset more than a technology [22].'

Agent-based models are natural representations in social sciences [15] and thus many ideas stem from this area [22]. More generally, agent-based models are well-suited for systems with heterogeneous, autonomous and pro-active actors where individual variability cannot be neglected [120, 27, 83]. Furthermore, interaction between agents is usually regarded to be essential [27, 68].

Recalling the difference between a model and its simulation, it is now straight-forward to define the term of a multi-agent simulation:

Definition 7 (Multi-agent simulation) A *multi-agent simulation* is the simulation of an agent-based model. □

Similar terms frequently used in literature are: agent-based modeling and simulation (ABMS), multi-agent simulation (MAS), individual-based modeling (IBM), agent-based modeling (ABM), agent-based simulation (ABS). This thesis uses the term agent-based modeling and simulation (if only the model itself is referred to, the clause *and simulation* is omitted).

Although multi-agent *simulations* and multi-agent *systems* share many ideas (and are both abbreviated as MAS), it is important to distinguish precisely between these two terms. The main difference is that multi-agent simulations take place in a simulated world, whereas multi-agent systems are usually considered to have interactions with the real world.

2.2.2 Agent architecture

So far, only the characteristics of an agent itself have been described. Additionally, the internal structure and operation of an agent is

important as it defines how an agent pursues and finally achieves its
desired objectives.

Definition 8 (Agent architecture) An *agent architecture* specifies
how the construction of an agent can be decomposed into the construction of a set of component modules and how these modules should be
made to interact (cp. [13, 85, 90]).   □

By this definition, the agent architecture defines the internal structure
of an agent, the component modules of an agent, their behavior and
interactions [39, p. 447]. On an abstract level, the internal structure
of an agent always consists of three main components [21, p. 10]:

• Sensor interface
  The sensor interface enables an agent to perceive the environment
  it is situated in.

• Effector interface
  The effector interface enables an agent to interact with the environment and to actively pursue its goals.

• Reasoner
  The reasoner is an internal component of the agent for processing
  the data perceived by the sensors, for decision making and for
  controlling effectors.

With respect to a specific agent architecture each of these components
has to be detailed further, e. g., the reasoner of an agent architecture
might include a knowledge base, workflow monitor, or planner [21,
p. 10]. In summary, an agent architecture defines how sensor data
(perceptions) and a possible internal state of an agent determine the
next actions (effector outputs) and the future internal state of an
agent [85]. This mapping of any given sequence of perceptions to an
action is also referred to as *agent function* [112, p. 33].

For classifying agent architectures, various approaches have been
suggested. According to Genesereth and Nilsson two general agent
architectures may be distinguished [39]:

- *Tropistic agents* are characterized by the fact that they do not possess a model of the world they are acting in. Therefore, behavior of tropistic agents is at any point in time completely defined by their current surroundings and actual sensor inputs [39, p. 448].

- In contrast to tropistic agents, *hysteretic agents* make use of an internal state, i. e., they keep track of external states and their sensor inputs and can use this knowledge later on for their choice of an action [39, p. 454].

This distinction is in good agreement with the classification by Sloman [123] who added but one more class:

- *Reactive agents* abstract of internal states and react directly to their sensor inputs.

- *Deliberative agents* make use of an explicit mental representation of their perceptions and follow (more or less) sophisticated planning procedures to choose their next action.

- *Reflective agents* are additionally capable of reflecting previous choices and are learning from the outcomes of previous actions.

Besides these clear-cut classes *hybrid* and *layered* agent architectures are wide-spread, aiming to combine multiple mechanisms to utilize the particular benefits [149], [135, p. 335ff.].

2.2.3 Relationships with other modeling paradigms

Characterizing modeling paradigms, the clearest distinction can be made between macroscopic modeling approaches (e. g., using differential equations or System Dynamics) and microscopic modeling approaches like agent-based modeling and simulation [68, 22, 27]. Macroscopic models abstract from individual system components and use high-level representations of the system under investigation. In contrast, microscopic models use a very fine-grained representation of a system and explicitly take into account individual characteristics and behavior of system components.

A comparison of agent-based modeling with established modeling techniques (e. g., cellular automata or queueing networks) can be found in [71]. Another approach in microscopic modeling is object-oriented simulation which has its roots in the 1960s [20, 62]. Basically, 'an object-oriented simulation consists of a set of objects that interact with each other over time' [62]. There are many commonalities between object-oriented simulation and agent-based modeling (like classes of similar entities, encapsulation of data and methods) [62, 20], [36, p. 45f.]. Nevertheless, there are also some differences, although mainly on a conceptual level. Within object-oriented simulations the simulated entities are usually not modeled using mentalistic concepts (e. g., beliefs, desires, intentions), the notion of space is less stressed, and objects are typically purely reactive (in contrast to autonomously acting agents) [27].

A precise distinction between agent-based modeling and object-oriented simulation cannot be made. In a way, agent-based modeling is more advanced on the conceptual level with ideas like autonomous agents, variable interactions and decision-making autonomy [68]. At the same time, each agent-based model uses a lot of ideas originally developed in the context of object-oriented simulation. Therefore, agent-based modeling 'is not the same as object-oriented simulation, but the object-oriented paradigm is a useful basis for agent modeling, as an agent can be considered a selfdirected object with the additional capability of action choice' [83].

Within the context of discrete event simulation several modeling views are common (e. g., process view or activity view). Similarly, agent-based modeling may be considered as another modeling view for describing a system under investigation. Therefore agent-based modeling is not something completely new but rather provides a new mindset.

Discrete event simulation uses events as central element, where events happen at a specific point in time and trigger state changes. The central notion of agent-based modeling is the agent and agents are supposed to be heterogeneous, active entities with individual behavior. Accordingly, agent-based modeling focusses on the behavior of single agents and their interactions with each other [27, 68, 120]. Discrete event simulation is primarily organized around objects and their state changes when an event occurs, while agent-based modeling puts the main focus on the behavior and actions of the agents. Models for discrete event simulations can be quite hard to understand (e. g., due to the fact that event routines related to an object are scattered throughout the model and that the control flow between the event routines may not be directly visible) and can therefore also be quite complicated to extend. Agent-based models on the other hand often provide a very natural representation of the system under investigation (e. g., with respect to the behavior of individuals, learning, interaction and spatial aspects) and offer a high scalability (both in the number of agents and in the complexity of their behavior) [83, 27].

In summary, agent-based modeling and simulation, object-oriented simulation and discrete event simulation use a different terminology and mindset for describing conceptual models and formal models of a system under investigation while the executable models derived from those may be undistinguishable.

2.2.4 Benefits and drawbacks of agent-based modeling and simulation

Agent-based modeling and simulation should not be seen as something completely new, but more as a new mindset which combines a lot of ideas already in use for a long time, with a strong emphasis on the notion of agents [27, 23]:

> 'Aspects of agent-based simulation (ABS) have been used by DoD analysts for years. The new concepts are the term agent and a few aspects of ABS—specifically the representation of knowledge and behavior. In addition, with ABS, there has been an emphasis on using simulations that are relatively low-resolution with respect to traditional methods.' [25]

Nevertheless, the following benefits compared to other modeling paradigms are frequently associated with agent-based modeling and simulation:

- Agent-based modeling allows a natural and often very intuitive, structure preserving modeling and implementation of the system under investigation [68, 22, 83, 27]. Furthermore, it is often more easy to describe the behavior of single agents and provide necessary data than to describe the behavior of the overall system.

- Agent-based modeling has the power to demonstrate emergent phenomena which are fundamentally a multiresolution concept. In other words, agent-based modeling allows a comparatively easy integration of different levels of modeling and observation [68, 15, 120], [84, 113]. This fits well to the fact that agent-based model development (and calibration) is often based on more fine-grained data as input compared to other modeling approaches [83].

- Agent-based modeling is flexible and provides high scalability. The level of detail within a model can be adjusted quite easily as agent-based modeling provides a natural framework for tuning the complexity of the agents (e. g., behavior, degree of rationality, ability to learn and evolve, and rules of interactions). Furthermore, agent-based models inherently support parallel and distributed simulation execution and promise a high degree of maintainability as well as extensibility [22, 83, 27, 23, 68].

In summary, building upon 'proven, highly successful techniques such as discrete event simulation and object-oriented programming, agent-based modeling leverages these and other techniques as much as possible to produce returns more directly and quickly' [93, p. 5f.].

Although the idea of agent-based modeling and simulation is easy to grasp and understand, and an implementation is technically quite simple, two major drawbacks can be identified [68, 60]:

1. The relation of behavior on the micro-level (i. e., of single agents) to behavior of the overall model is extremely difficult to predict

(sometimes impossible) because of the possibility of emergent behavior. Due to this missing micro-macro-link, it is often difficult to choose the right level of detail for a model. This may lead to overly complex models requiring time-consuming and possibly erroneous calibration. Also, it is often unknown which behavior on the micro-level yields a known or desired behavior on the macro-level.

2. Agent-based modeling and simulation typically requires a higher computational effort (runtime, memory) than traditional methods. This is due to the more detailed modeling of behavior associated with microscopic models.

Weighing the pros and cons, agent-based modeling seems most promising when dealing with complex systems characterized by a large number of individually acting entities. The behavior of the entities and their interaction may be translated quite directly into an agent-based model. Compared to other modeling paradigms, this similarity (of structure and interaction) between the system under investigation and the model is probably the most notable aspect of agent-based models. Finally, the practical (not conceptual) application of multi-agent simulation is closely connected with the availability of sufficient computational power allowing to simulate large-scale microscopic models [83].

2.3 Related work

In the following subsections, currently existing approaches to (formally) specify agent-based models and their simulation are presented. Due to the amount of approaches and systems in the agent-based modeling and simulation domain, it is not possible to exhaustively present all of them. Instead, various selected approaches are presented which represent different ways of describing agent-based models. The first approach is a proposal by Klügl [69] for a formal framework for multi-agent simulations. The second approach was developed by Scheutz and Schermerhorn [114] and is especially interesting as it deals explicitly with parallel execution. The third approach was proposed in 1996 by Ferber and Müller [33] and has also spawned several follow-up developments. After presenting these three approaches the agent-object-relationship model by Wagner and two further relevant approaches are presented briefly.

2.3.1 Klügl (2007)

Motivation

Klügl argues that one of the reasons hindering the wide-spread use of multi-agent simulation (especially outside universities) is the lack of a formal basis. This leads to missing standards of specification and documentation with the consequence of missing reproducibility. Furthermore, a 'generic formal framework for representing agent-based simulation would also support differentiation between agent-based approaches and traditional microscopic ones' [69]. As it is also one of the key challenges (according to Klügl) to point out advantages of agent-based simulation in contrast to other paradigms, such a formal framework would be very useful.

In summary, Klügl points out that 'there is no framework that fully pins down which elements a Multi-Agent Simulation Model consists of and what relations might exist between these elements' [69].

Outline of the framework

Klügl distinguishes between structural aspects and processes respectively dynamics. Let $E = \{e_1, e_2, \ldots, e_n\}$ be the set of environmental entities, i. e., the set of objects that exist in an environment. Together with the set $P = \{p_1, p_2, \ldots, p_m\}$ of environmental properties the complete physical configuration of a multi-agent simulation is given as $PCON = E \cup P$. The set of all possible states of an entity e is denoted by SE_e, the cartesian product ES of all SEs gives the set of all possible states of all entities and properties. The initial configuration is then given by a function $initializeConfig : PCON \to ES$.

Based on the set of entities E, the following two functions are defined:

$$embody : A \rightarrow E \qquad (2.1)$$

$$identify : R \rightarrow E \qquad (2.2)$$

These two functions associate an agent $a \in A$ respectively a resource $r \in R$ with one of the entities. Each entity is mapped either to an agent or to a resource. Each agent a is further associated with a set M_a of mental properties (e.g., beliefs, desires, ...) with possible states SA_a. Klügl explicitly points out 'once more the separation between mental and physical properties' [69] of the agents.

Due to an explicit treatment of the environment, Klügl makes a clear distinction between environmental dynamics and agent-related dynamics. The environmental update therefore is represented by the functions

$$ressUpdate_r : SE_r \times T \rightarrow SE_r \qquad (2.3)$$

$$propUpdate_p : ES \times T \rightarrow SE_p \qquad (2.4)$$

which update a resource r respectively a global property p (T denoting the simulation time).

The agent-related dynamics, i.e., the agents activities, depend heavily on the previously given definitions. As these definitions are rather high-level, the description of the agents activities is also rather high-level and mainly defined by an internal status update function

$$mentalUpdate : S_a \rightarrow S_a \qquad (2.5)$$

where S_a denotes the complete possible state set of an agent a (i.e., $S_a = SE_a \times SA_a$). As *situatedness* is one of the defining criteria for an agent, two more functions are defined: *percept* and *act*. The *percept* function

$$percept_a : RU_a \times SE_a \rightarrow SE_a \qquad (2.6)$$

defines which information an agent a may perceive from its relevant individual environment RU_a and maps this information to the physical state of the agent. The behavior of an agent is then defined by the function

$$act_a : S_a \rightarrow ACT_a \qquad (2.7)$$

where ACT_a denotes the set of possible actions of an agent a. As an agent can only control its effectors, but not the effects of its action in the environment, Klügl separates (in accordance with [33], see also sec. 2.3.3) the agents actions from the environmental outcome. Therefore, the function

$$execute : ACT_{a_1} \times \cdots \times ACT_{a_n} \rightarrow ES \qquad (2.8)$$

of the environment actually computes the effects of all attempted actions.

The global state set $GS = ES \times MS$ (with $MS = SA_1 \times \cdots \times SA_i$) is defined as the set of all possible physical states and mental states. A simulation starts with a given state $gs(0) \in GS$ (usually determined by the $initConfig$ function) and consists of the iterated application of the update functions defined by the model onto this state. The result is a sequence $(gs(t)_{t \in T})$ of states indexed and ordered according to the simulation time, the so-called simulation trajectory.

Strengths and weaknesses

The formal framework proposed by Klügl is to be understood as a first attempt, although unfortunately no further work on this framework was published and development seems to have come to a stop. Besides, there are several strengths and weaknesses. The framework aims to provide a formally grounded terminology about agent-based models and shows the model structure and dynamics in a quite concise way, making consequent use of a rigorous mathematical notation. The major drawbacks are:

1. Insufficient integration of simulation time

2. Only a weak model of interactions

3. Compactness and conciseness

As Klügl points out, especially 'the simulation time is not integrated with sufficient detail. Thus, synchronization aspects remain vague. However, synchronization is often the technically most difficult aspect in implementing an agent-based simulation' [69]. This assessment is underpinned by the quite vague definition of a simulation execution, omitting detailed information whether all agents have to act simultaneously in a stepwise manner or if asynchronous actions are possible.

Furthermore, Klügl remarks that 'only a weak model of interfaces and interactions is given' [69]. At this point, it should be noted that the approach of Klügl provides a potential solution for handling conflicting actions of multiple agents (using an influence-reaction approach). Somehow related to this aspect is the need 'to tackle the dilemma between conciseness of the framework and clear separation of concerns' [69]. In its current status, the proposed level of detail is not sufficient to reproduce the model, resulting in the conclusion that it 'is not yet sufficient for compact (and concise) documentation of even simple models' [69].

A major problem seems to be the close dependency of the definition of the agents activities and the definition of a simulation. The definition of a simulation as a series of state transitions assumes a synchronization of all actions (and therefore of all agents). Furthermore, this implies a time-stepped execution which in turn demands the modeling of the agents activities in terms of these steps. In this way, the definition of an agent and the definition of a simulation are coupled very closely, imposing unnecessary modeling constraints.

A further drawback results from the choice to handle actions according to the influence-reaction approach. The delegation of computing effects of desired actions to the environment can be seen quite controversary. On the one hand, it is an easy solution to this problem, on the other hand it is usually not the task of the environment to calculate the outcome of actions of agents acting in this environment. A more

detailed analysis of the influence-reaction approach will be given in
Section 2.3.3, and an exhaustive discussion as well as more details on
the role of the environment are given in Section 2.4. Summing up, the
framework proposed by Klügl provides formal descriptions of many
ideas which are central to agent-based modeling. Unfortunately, the
lack of a well-integrated simulation time and the time-stepped execution are great disadvantages (especially as no further development
takes place).

2.3.2 Scheutz, Schermerhorn (2006)

Motivation

Scheutz and Schermerhorn state that 'it is very difficult ... to utilize
the potential parallelism present in many agent-based models for
running parts of the models in parallel' [114]. They believe, that
'an algorithm that can automatically and dynamically distribute a
given agent-based model over a dynamically changing set of CPUs
... would be of great utility' [114]. They also point out very clearly,
that a prerequisite for the definition of any mechanism for automatic
parallelization or load distribution is a 'formal description of the
notion of *agent-based model*' [114], as otherwise all approaches are
only applicable and valid for specific model instances.

  Therefore, their motivation for defining a formal model of a multi-
agent simulation is derived from the intention to design algorithms for
automatic parallelization of multi-agent simulations defined within
their proposed framework.

Outline of the framework

In short, the framework defined by Scheutz and Schermerhorn char-
acterizes 'a simulation of an agent-based model as a computational
process that starts in some initial condition and then updates the

agents' states and environmental states over time' [114]. The agent-based model $\mathcal{M}$ is defined as 6-tuple:

$$\mathcal{M} = (Env_{\mathcal{M}}, GS_{\mathcal{M}}, Loc_{\mathcal{M}}, Ent_{\mathcal{M}}, Init_{\mathcal{M}}, Cond_{\mathcal{M}}) \qquad (2.9)$$

with $Env_{\mathcal{M}}$ as n-dimensional environment, $GS_{\mathcal{M}}$ as the set of global environmental states, $Loc_{\mathcal{M}}$ as a set of locations in the environment, $Ent_{\mathcal{M}}$ as a set of entity types, $Init_{\mathcal{M}}$ as a set of initial configurations and $Cond_{\mathcal{M}}$ as a set of conditions defining the final configurations. The set of all possible configurations determined by the model $\mathcal{M}$ is denoted by $Cfg_{\mathcal{M}}$.

A single entity $E = (B_E, C_E, U_E)$ consists of a body B_E, a controller C_E and an update function U_E. The body represents the physical properties of an entity (e. g., available sensors and actuators, geometry, location of the entity, . . .). The controller represents some kind of internal state and is mainly defined by an update function as a mapping from internal states and input to internal states and output. The update function U_E combines update functions for physical properties and the update function of the controller.

In order to define exactly what is meant by the term *simulation of an agent-based model*, Scheutz and Schermerhorn define the terms *successor configuration* and *model update function*. Roughly speaking, if $C_i \in Cfg_{\mathcal{M}}$ is a configuration, then the successor configuration C_{i+1} can be computed as $C_{i+1} = U_{\mathcal{M}}(C_i)$, where $U_{\mathcal{M}}$ denotes the model update function (basically the union of the entity update functions U_E and the update functions for the environmental locations U_L). With this in mind, a simulation is defined as follows:

'A simulation of a model $\mathcal{M}$ (as defined above) is a finite sequence of configurations $C_0, C_1, \ldots, C_{final}$ starting with an initial configuration $C_0 \in Init_{\mathcal{M}}$ and ending in a final configuration C_{final}, where all $C_i \in Cfg_{\mathcal{M}}$ and only C_{final} satisfies the conditions for a final configuration.' [114]

Therefore, simulations defined in this way are consequently deterministic and reproducible from the chosen initial states.

Strengths and weaknesses

As Scheutz and Schermerhorn are focused on parallelizing the computation of the simulation of an agent-based model, the framework is just developed and used to describe and verify their load distribution algorithms. Unfortunately, as Scheutz and Schermerhorn just published one article [114] on this topic, some important aspects remain open.

The aspect of greatest interest in the context of this thesis is the decision to assume a time-stepped execution of the simulation model with fixed time increments. Besides the remark that 'to their knowledge, all agent-based model simulation environments capable of distributed simulation implement some form of stepwise synchronization mechanism' [114] similar to the one they proposed, they do not motivate their decision in any way. Given the numerous arguments for and against time-stepped simulation with fixed time increments, especially when compared to discrete event simulation (e. g., inefficiency due to long idle periods, strictly periodical state updates), a more detailed explanation for choosing a time-stepped execution of the model is missing.

A further important aspect concerns the resolution of conflicting actions of multiple agents which is not explained in detail. They do not mention this problem at all, although it can be assumed that the various update functions are responsible for this task. Again, as this aspect is central and can be a potential bottleneck (as simply verifying all possible agent interactions requires quadratic runtime), it would be of interest how it is handled. This aspect is even more interesting as the proposed load distribution algorithms make explicit use of the *update independence* of the entities. In a way, Scheutz and Schermerhorn deal only with update-independent entities, i. e., with entities which do not conflict with each other during a simulation step.

Besides these drawbacks, a highly appreciated result of Scheutz and Schermerhorn is that they can proof the correctness of their load balancing algorithm. This feature of being able to proof the (result-)equivalence of sequential and parallel execution of a multi-agent simulation is highly desirable for various reasons and should be regarded as essential when parallelizing any simulation.

2.3.3 Ferber, Müller (1996) and Weyns, Holvoet (2003)

Motivation

Moving from multi-agent simulation to multi-agent systems, *situatedness* and autonomy remain two of the main aspects of any such system. Resembling the current state in formalizing a multi-agent simulation, Weyns and Holvoet state that 'comparatively few work has been done to specify conceptual models for multi-agent systems in a formalized way' [143].

Based on the model by Ferber and Müller which separates what agents do and how the environment reacts upon this, Weyns and Holvoet point out the limitations and come up with an own approach. In the following, the model of Ferber and Müller as well as its limitations are described, followed by the approach of Weyns and Holvoet.

Influence-reaction approach of Ferber and Müller

The influence-reaction approach of Ferber and Müller was introduced in 1996. Its key idea is a 'clear distinction between influences, which are produced by agents' behaviour, and the reaction of the environment' [33]. Influences generally result from an agents internal behavior and are attempts to execute some specific task. On the other hand, reactions are the product of the combined influences of all agents within a certain area of the environment.

A similar approach is proposed by Goodwin [46] who distinguishes between commands and interactions. Whereas commands are totally under control of an agent and represent its attempt to alter the environment, interactions represent the actual outcome in the environment. Although the basic principle is very similar, Goodwin mentions only vaguely the use of commands and interactions to model failing actions or conflicting actions of multiple agents.

Ferber and Müller develop a consistent formal theory, which is sufficient for dealing with complex interactions between agents and the environment. A drawback of their original theory is that it 'is limited to synchronous descriptions of the multiagent systems evolutions' [33]. This is due to the cause that Ferber and Müller assume that a multi-agent system may be described by repetitive execution of a *cycle*-function. Each cycle consists of collecting the influences produced by the agents as well as the dynamics of the environment and computing the reactions. As pointed out by Ferber and Müller [33] themselves as well as by Weyns and Holvoet [143], acting in such a *lock step* manner does not match the autonomous behavior of agents and limits scalability.

Action model of Weyns and Holvoet

Based on the work of Ferber and Müller, Weyns and Holvoet propose an alternative to the centralized synchronization model in the form of an action model based on regional synchronization. With respect to the approach of Ferber and Müller they point out that 'all agents of the multi-agent system act at one global pace, i. e., the agents are globally synchronized' [144]. There are two major difficulties with this: Firstly, global synchronization implies a centralized control of the multi-agent system (respectively simulation), which is in general a very undesirable requirement (as it is usually in contrast to the nature of multi-agent systems, which are often distributed and without centralized control). Secondly, since the influences of all agents are treated as if they happen at the same point in time, the total number of possible interactions is of the order of $O(n^2)$ for a model with n agents and thus limits scalability.

The basic idea of Weyns and Holvoet to overcome these difficulties is to constrain simultaneous actions to groups of agents which are only regionally synchronized. Different groups of agents can therefore act asynchronously. Figure 2.3 compares the approaches of Ferber and Müller (F-M) and Weyns and Holvoet (W-H). In the F-M model the reaction is computed as soon as all influences are collected. This view

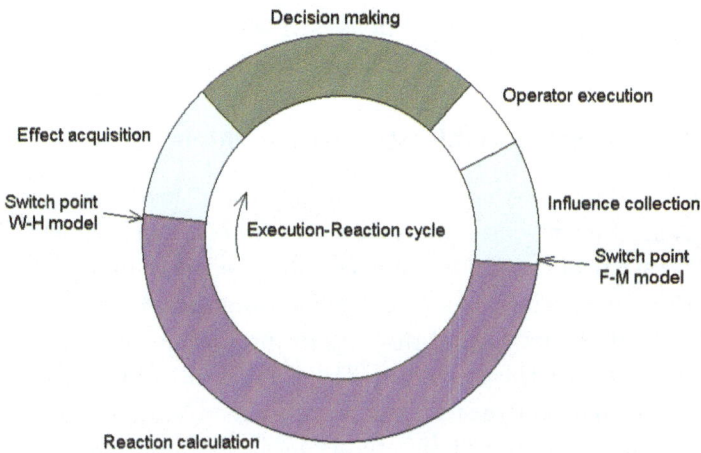

Figure 2.3: Comparison of execution-reaction cycles of Ferber and Müller (F-M) and Weyns and Holvoet (W-H) [144].

on the system evolution is indicated by the 'Switch point F-M model'. In contrast, Weyns and Holvoet propose an agent-centered view and shift the switch point after the reaction calculation. Therefore, each agent may decide for itself when to start his cycle.

Strengths and weaknesses

The influence-reaction approach and its extension by regional synchronization is an interesting way of handling multiple concurrent actions of various agents and determining the resulting overall effect. Weyns and Holvoet point out mainly three open issues of their proposed model, namely dealing with time, the problem of the synchronization of agent activities and other dynamics in the environment, as well as the direct communication between agents. Most of these issues are connected with physical activities and therefore apply to multi-agent systems but not necessarily multi-agent simulations.

The speedup gained by regional synchronization depends on the size of the regions and the average number of agents per region. A

well-designed composition of regions is therefore necessary to improve
autonomy of the agents and enhance scalability.

2.3.4 DEVS and variable structure models

The DEVS (discrete event system specification) formalism allows the
description of event-based systems in a formal way [151]. DEVS supports hierarchical modeling, thus coupling existing models to create
more complex models. As Uhrmacher points out, 'original DEVS
assumes, as do other formal discrete event simulation approaches, a
static structure of the system' [131], [17]. This static model structure is in sharp contrast to the very idea of agent-based models,
which assumes lots of entities interacting in manifold, not completely
predetermined ways and changing their behavior pattern if necessary.

Although DEVS provides a strict formalism and is well-understood
for modeling discrete event systems, the possibilities to describe agent-
based models using DEVS seem limited. This is due to several reasons:
First and foremost, it seems hardly possible, if at all, to describe all
possible changes in the structure of a model in advance. As almost
all aspects of an agent-based model (like the environment or the
agents and their embedding) are subject to manifold changes, the
chances of defining all these structural changes in advance are low.
Secondly, agent-based models are inherently modeling the micro-level
and depend heavily on the communication and interaction between the
agents. Explicitly modeling all possible communication and interaction
relations between the agents of a specific model is about as hard as
defining all possible structural changes.

Therefore, the current assessment is that DEVS is not ideally suited
for the description of agent-based models as a whole. On the other
hand, DEVS may be well suited for describing the behavior of single
agents. Furthermore, the strict distinction made by DEVS between
model, abstract simulator and actually implemented simulator is
worth mentioning.

With the limitations of DEVS in mind, several extensions of the
original DEVS formalism have been proposed to support models with

variable and dynamic structure [132, 17, 131]. For modeling the micro- and macro-level of a system, Multi-Level-DEVS (*ml*-DEVS) is proposed [133, 124] which connects the micro-level (i. e., a single agent) with the macro-level. Therefore, *ml*-DEVS (or some adaptation of it taking variable structures into account) may be used for formally describing an agent-based model. The major drawback of DEVS (and the various variants of DEVS) is that the modeling is not very intuitive and the resulting models become hard to understand quite fast.

2.3.5 Agent-Object-Relationship Simulation

The Agent-Object-Relationship (AOR) modeling is an agent-oriented approach for conceptual modeling of organizations and organizational information systems, taking into account both static and dynamic aspects [136]. In [139, 137] it is shown that this approach can also be used for specifying simulation models.

The Agent-Object-Relationship Simulation (AORS) is developed as an extension of traditional discrete event simulation. An AORS simulation model consists of a model of the environment, a model for each involved agent and a specification of the initial states for the environment and for all agents. A time-stepped execution with fixed time increments per cycle is assumed [137, 138]. Based on the ideas of AOR modeling, the *Agent-Object-Relationship (AOR) Simulation Language* is developed. It consists of an abstract model (described in UML) and an according XML Schema defining the actual syntax.

The Agent-Object-Relationship Simulation (AORS) takes into account many important aspects of agent-based modeling and simulation. Most notably the clear distinction between a simulation model and its execution stands out. The simulation model can be expressed formally (following the specified XML Schema) and independently of an actual simulator executing it. The actual simulators in turn are based on an abstract simulator. Thus, all parts are clearly separated from each other and each part is based on a solid conceptual specification.

Two drawbacks are identified: First, although the simulation model itself is formalized (via XML Schema), the execution of a simulation is defined in a textual way only [137, 107]. Second, the AORS approach assumes a simulation execution with fixed time increments.

2.3.6 Further related work

De Vries et al. (2001)

De Vries et al. present a model of agents with a flexible cycle of sensing, reasoning and acting. They explicitly deal with *actions with duration* and *true concurrency*, which means that concurrent actions are treated as happening simultaneously [30].

Right at the beginning, De Vries et al. state that though 'interaction is a key concept for agents, these issues are not properly treated in many agent programming languages' [30]. In the following they state furthermore that 'typically, actions are atomic and take zero time, events from the environment aren't explicitly modelled and interference or synergy of actions is impossible' [30]. Their model aims to address these issues.

They notice that most agents perform some kind of *sense-reason-act cycle*. Therefore they propose a flexible execution cycle consisting of reasoning and interaction, with observation being just a special kind of interaction. The only requirement imposed on this cycle is that in every iteration the reasoning precedes the interaction. Furthermore, they point out that the agents have to observe their environment explicitly and that their perception can differ from the true state of the environment.

In order to allow actions with duration, actions are composed of atomic sub-actions consuming one time unit each. Based on this approach, parallel execution is defined for various cases (parallel internal actions, parallel external actions, parallel internal and external actions). In this way, De Vries et al. completely abstract from the inner functioning of the agents and focus on concurrent execution.

They conclude by stating that their model incorporates five important aspects, which are usually not all handled in other models: a dynamic world with events, actions of observation, actions with duration, group- and individual actions, incorporation of true concurrency.

On the positive side, De Vries et al. provide a well-defined model that takes care of a lot of problems encountered in other approaches. A very important aspect is that they distinguish between 'a local semantics for individual agent programs and a global semantics which composes the local behaviours of the agents and events happening in the world into a global system behaviour' [30]. On the other hand, they restrict the agents to the iterated execution of some behavior specification and use a time-stepped execution with fixed time increments. The disadvantage of this approach is that all parts of the model (i. e., agents and environment) have to be described using the same level of granularity, which will not be optimal in all cases. Furthermore, this leads to a very close coupling of model components and thus complicates the reuse of these components within other models. Another negative aspect of this approach is that modeling issues (behavior of the agents) are coupled to execution issues (time steps of fixed size) which limits adaptability, flexibility and reuse.

Ke, Hu (2006)

Ke and Hu point out that 'concurrent behaviors turn out to be very important under the multi-agent system circumstances' [66]. They furthermore point out that the approach of De Vries et al. does not contain 'solutions to the non-deterministic and behavioral conflicts induced by true concurrency' [66]. Therefore, they present a concurrent agent model aiming at the characteristics of concurrent behavior in multi-agent systems. In sharp contrast to the models presented in the previous sections, the model of Ke and Hu is based on ideas of the fields of modal and temporal logic.

Somehow similar to De Vries et al. the model of Ke and Hu makes use of two distinct time scales: macro-time and micro-time. In their model, an action's duration endures at least one macro-time segment.

While all aspects of concurrency are described on macro-time level, concurrent actions are interleaved on the micro-time level. Therefore, the model of Ke and Hu suffers from the same disadvantages already mentioned for the model of De Vries et al. in the previous section (especially stepwise execution and close coupling of components).

2.3.7 Summary

This section summarizes the common aspects of the presented approaches to describe agent-based models and the further presented approaches as well as the differences between them. Although the models and approaches presented cover a wide range and are not necessarily comparable to each other, there are a few aspects which all these models have in common:

- Situatedness of the agents and importance of the environment

- Distinction of active and passive entities

- Distinction between intended actions and the actual outcome

- Assumption of time-stepped execution

Besides these common aspects, all presented approaches suffer from certain weaknesses. To be clear, not all of the approaches suffer from all of these weaknesses, instead the list is meant as a more or less complete account of the identified weaknesses:

- Unclear distinction between model and simulation engine

- Insufficient definition of simulation time and time-advancement mechanism

- No consideration of concurrent and conflicting actions

- Insufficient consideration of the environment

The above mentioned aspects are discussed in detail in the following subsections.

Common aspects

The common aspects of the presented approaches towards a formal framework for multi-agent simulation can be regarded as essential aspects in the design of such a framework.

Situatedness within the environment   First of all, the importance of the environment is regularly emphasized. This is somehow intuitively clear, as the common definition of an agent usually contains the concept of *situatedness* (e. g., [112, p. 32f.], [81, p. 7f.], [1, p. 5]). Especially Klügl advocates for explicit modeling of the environment and favors the ideas laid down in [52]. Another common aspect is that most approaches consider various types of entities within the model. An obvious distinction is given by Klügl in separating the entities (mutually exclusive) into agents and resources.

Distinction of active and passive entities   The distinction between active and passive entities (i. e., agents and objects) is part of all approaches. Furthermore, a very common aspect is the separation of an agent into its body on the one hand and its mind on the other hand [114, 69]. Consequently, the body or the physical properties of an agent are perceptible by other agents, whereas the mind of an agent is *private* in a sense, that usually just the agent itself has access to it.

The passive entities ususally represent some objects from the real world and are therefore associated with a couple of defining properties which may well change respectively be altered during a simulation. The main difference to the agents is that the passive entities do not exhibit any behavior and do not actively influence a simulation in any way.

Distinction between intended actions and actual outcome   The importance of differentiating between the *intended action* of an agent and the *execution of the action* is stressed by many authors. The reason for this is that 'one must accept, that the agent itself can only control its effectors, but not the effects of its action in the environment' [69, p. 9]. This distinction is especially 'important in modeling situations, where an entity's controller might attempt to achieve a state that is inconsistent with the environmental state' [114, p. 1040].

Assumption of time-stepped execution Although not always explicitly mentioned, most approaches make use of a time-stepped execution with fixed time increments [24]. The definition of a simulation of Scheutz and Schermerhorn explicitly covers this time-stepped execution and further implies that all agents are executed in each time step and that no action can happen in between these time steps. Implicitly assumed in this approach is the fact, that all actions the agents are able to execute always take exactly one time step duration for execution.

Klügl defines a simulation quite similar in terms of model configurations and 'the iterated application of the update functions' [69, p. 15]. Due to a missing formal description, the definition of a simulation remains quite vague and the time-stepped execution is not mentioned explicitly.

Weaknesses

Although the approaches presented have a lot in common, they also have weaknesses and lack several features.

Unclear distinction between model and simulation engine Many approaches do not provide clear definitions of the model (i. e., environment, agents and their behavior), the simulation of a model and the actual execution of the simulation by a specific simulation engine. The approach of Scheutz and Schermerhorn as well as the Agent-Object-Relationship Simulation are notable exceptions.

The absence of a clear distinction leads to fuzzy definitions and hinders the future development as well as it puts unnecessary limitations to the development of multi-agent simulations within (large) teams. Furthermore, the unclear basis complicates the development of alternative simulation engines which adhere to a common set of specifications (e. g., a sequential simulation engine or a massively parallel simulation engine, capable of executing exactly the same model).

Insufficient definition of simulation time and time-advancement mechanism Many approaches miss a consistent and well-defined description of simulation time or a definition of the time-advancement mechanism. Closely related to this is the vague definition of synchronization aspects in the approaches of Klügl and Scheutz and Schermerhorn. As 'synchronization is often the technically most difficult aspect in implementing an agent-based simulation' [69, p. 22], the missing accuracy and clarity in this point is a major drawback of these two approaches. Furthermore, both approaches do not specify whether the simulation steps are all of the same length (in matters of time), and both approaches do not make any statement on the granularity or atomicity of the actions of the agents. This means, it is unclear whether each action has to be executed within a single simulation step or within multiple simulation steps. Therefore, it is unclear how much time actions consume or if the agents behavior is based on some kind of *atomic actions*.

Any answer to this question will also have to deal with the problem of conflicting actions. The approaches of De Vries et al. and Ke/Hu both deal with the matter of actions with duration and have further in common that they distinguish between a macro-time and a micro-time scale. Actions are commonly defined on the macro-time level while the concurrent execution usually takes place on the micro-time level. Therefore these two approaches provide a useful starting point for integrating this missing aspect.

The whole area of interference of actions is treated only very sparse in the presented approaches, except for the approaches of De Vries et al. and Ke/Hu that may thus provide useful starting points.

No consideration of concurrent and conflicting actions Given the parallel execution of multiple agents, there will always be the case, that the actions of two or more agents will conflict. This presents multiple challenges: At first, possible conflicts have to be detected (e. g., depending on the agents locations or on the type of action the agents want to execute). After detection of possible conflicts, consequences of these conflicts have to be determined and the influences onto the agents desired behavior have to be computed. Finally, the actions and events resulting from conflicts have to be executed and made perceptible to the agents (both, the agents directly involved as well as the agents in sensor range of this event).

Scheutz/Schermerhorn as well as Klügl put this aspect aside and *hide* these details within their respective model update functions. But as this topic bears a lot of information for the execution of a simulation and is directly connected to the (above mentioned) aspect of the atomicity of actions and simulation time needed for the execution of an action, this topic of conflicting actions seems to be too important not to be considered in the definition of a reference model for an agent-based simulation.

2.4 The role of the environment in agent-based models

As mentioned several times in the previous sections, the environment usually plays a crucial role in a multi-agent simulation [13, 146]. In order to avoid confusion and because of a multitude of different and sometimes unclear ways of dealing with the environment, especially in the closely related fields of multi-agent *simulation* and multi-agent *systems*, a precise definition of the term is necessary.

First of all, it is important to distinguish between the simulated environment and the simulation environment. In short, the *simulated environment* is a goal-directed abstraction of the original environment and thus part of the model itself, whereas the *simulation environment* provides the infrastructure necessary for running the simulation [70].

Although this distinction is highly desirable, it is not realized in many available simulation applications [70]. Furthermore, it is important to stress this distinction, as many publications especially in the field of multi-agent systems do not emphasize it and use the term *environment* in various contexts [146, 95].

The following subsections deal with the simulated environment unless explicitly stated otherwise. As 'the simulated environment is part of the model itself, it should be specified with at least the same amount of carefulness as the simulated multi agent system' [70]. Nevertheless, 'most researchers neglect to integrate the environment as a primary abstraction ... or minimize its responsibilities' [146, 147]. Keeping this in mind, a large amount of issues regarding the environment itself and the relations of agents and the environment still needs to be solved.

2.4.1 Definition and properties

The agents of a multi-agent simulation, representing some active entities of the system under investigation, are usually placed within some environment and their actions are therefore depending on and limited to this environment [95]. To put it differently, 'the simulated environment contains what the agents may perceive and manipulate' [70]. In a more general sense, the environment denotes the common space in which various types of entities are interacting (either active or passive). Active entities are commonly represented by the agents, whereas passive entities can be used to represent arbitrary objects within the simulated environment which do not exhibit any behavior. Besides these entities, the environment may carry some global state variables like overall temperature, also referred to as environmental properties [70, 52, 69].

The set of environmental entities can usually be partitioned into disjoint subsets (e. g., the above mentioned active and passive entities). Often the concept of embedding is used for relating agents to entities.

In this case a function maps the agent to the corresponding entity, which represents the tangible part (i. e., body) of the agent:

$$embody : agent \rightarrow entity \qquad (2.10)$$

In this way, embodiment is the central relation between agents and the environment [52, 69]. Some authors extend the scope of the environment even one step further and state that the environment not only consists of all the entities, 'but also those principles and processes under which the agents exist and communicate' [95].

Regarding the spatial aspect of an environment, usually no constraints are given and a partitioning is assumed to be possible, i. e., 'each agent environment can be thought of as a whole or it can be subdivided into discrete regions' [95]. Depending on the represented system under investigation, the environment may be non-spatial, discrete or continuous and a further distinction can be made between absolute and relative locality of the entities within the environment [70, 95].

2.4.2 Dynamics

As mentioned in the previous section, the simulated environment can be seen as consisting of environmental entities and environmental properties, e. g., overall temperature. Additionally, the environment may even have its own dynamics, e. g., temperature changes. Therefore, dynamics refers to the evolution of the simulated environment (environmental entities and properties) over time.

Similar to entities being either active or passive, also the environment itself can be characterized in this way: in contrast to a passive environment where all changes in the environment are reactions to some actions by the agents, an active environment possesses dynamics which are independent from the embedded agents actions and may change the state without some agent causing it [70] [147, 99, 100]. With respect to the previously mentioned embedding, not only agents can initiate activities but also entities not embodying any agent [70, 52].

The real environment is typically dynamic, meaning that the environment changes in ways beyond the agents' control. Therefore the dynamics should also be modeled explicitly as part of the simulated environment. The approach proposed in [52] is very similar to the approach proposed by Klügl (see Section 2.3.1), in fact the approach of Klügl is based on [52]. The authors advocate for the influence-reaction model and propose a formalism to model dynamic environments in multi-agent simulation.

Odell adapts the description of Parunak [99] and expresses the environment as a tuple *environment* = (*state, process*) with *state* denoting the complete state of the environment and *process* being an autonomously executing mapping that changes the environment's state. Autonomously executing means that the process runs without being invoked from any outside entity [95].

3 Parallel and distributed multi-agent simulation

This chapter gives an overview of basic terminology in the area of parallel and distributed multi-agent simulation and presents existing approaches and their limitations for parallel execution of multi-agent simulations.

3.1 Basic terminology

According to [36], the four main reasons to consider parallel and distributed execution of a simulation are:

1. Reduced execution time.

2. Geographical distribution.

3. Integrating simulators and simulation models that execute on machines from different manufacturers.

4. Fault tolerance.

As shown in Figure 3.1, hardware platforms providing multiple processors are divided broadly into two categories. Parallel computers are usually homogeneous machines which are connected by specialized interconnects to reduce latencies between the machines. On the other hand, distributed systems consist of geographically distributed, heterogeneous machines which are usually loosely coupled (sometimes only temporarily for a specific purpose).

The distinction between parallel and distributed computers is not clear-cut. A cluster or network of workstations may be classified

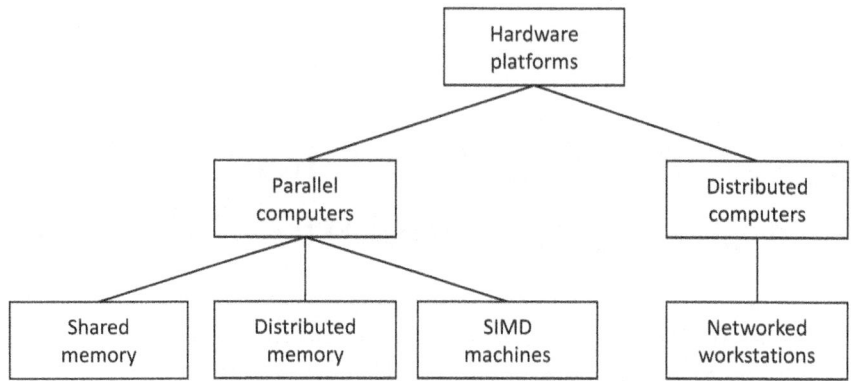

Figure 3.1: Taxonomy of important classes of parallel and distributed
computers [36].

as either distributed computer (because of the use of common-of-
the-shelf network hardware) or as parallel computer (because of the
close physical proximity of the machines) [36, p. 18f.]. The following
definitions are used in this thesis:

Definition 9 (Parallel simulation) *Parallel simulation* refers to
the concurrent, independent execution of a simulation model using
multiple threads, processors or computing nodes. Within this thesis,
this term does *not* refer to the time-parallel execution of multiple
independent simulations.   □

Definition 10 (Distributed simulation) *Distributed simulation*
refers to the execution of a simulation model using multiple, distributed
computing nodes. Usually the overall simulated model consists of
multiple interconnected simulation models executed by the available
computing nodes.   □

Parallel simulation is usually considered for improving performance
of the simulation execution (i. e., to reduce runtime) or for increasing
reliability of the simulation environment [49]. The common focus
of distributed simulation is to couple existing simulators. Therefore,

distributed simulation has to take into account many aspects of interoperability often unknown at design time. On the contrary, the requirements on a parallel simulation are generally well-known at design time. Although a parallel simulation may be implemented as a distributed system, all components of this system are generally designed and implemented in a coherent fashion. Therefore, parallel simulation avoids most of the interoperability pitfalls of distributed simulation.

The potential benefits of parallel and distributed simulation do not come for free. Typically, parallel simulation introduces the need for synchronization to ensure logical causality. The main problem regarding distributed simulation is to ensure interoperability between all simulation components.

3.2 Motivation and requirements with respect to multi-agent simulation

Agent-based models demonstrate an inherent parallelism as multiple agents are acting in parallel, thereby imposing a kind of natural decomposition [114, 6, 23, 78]. Unfortunately, this inherent parallelism is almost never exploited. This is due to the fact that exploiting this parallelism is usually very difficult for non-experts in parallel programming. Many existing approaches to parallelize the execution are also not generic but tailored to specific execution environments. Therefore, '... it would be particularly helpful if ABM researchers did not have to worry about the parallelization themselves, but rather could defer it to simulation software' [114].

Any approach to parallelize the execution of an agent-based simulation should fulfill the following requirements:

1. Transparency with respect to the executed model.

2. Consideration and exploitation of current technological trends (e. g., multi-core processors).

The first requirement essentially states that already available simulation models may be executed on a parallel simulation engine without the need of actually changing the simulation model. This requirement is important for several reasons:

- In order to support the model development process, it is highly desirable that the developer is able to develop and test the model using his local computing infrastructure. Also the sponsor and the subject matter experts should be able to execute the model (perhaps smaller in scale) on a regular desktop computer. Obviously, shifting the execution of the model to a multi-core or even multi-processor system running a parallelized simulation engine makes only sense if no changes of the model are required. The model development may be done locally (and perhaps decentralized), while the final simulation can be executed on an appropriate high-performance computer system.

- Testing as well as verification and validation of a model is a time- and resource-consuming task. If major changes of a model are necessary when executing it by a different simulation engine, the necessary quality assurance activities have to be carried out again (cp. [101, p. 190ff.], [125, 98]). The possibility to execute a model on different simulation engines can reduce this effort a lot as quality assurance has to be done only once for each model, independent of the simulation engine.

The *Transparency*-requirement is addressed by the GRAMS reference model. The reference model defines explicitly the components of an agent-based model as well as its execution. These definitions are implementation-independent and do not prescribe any specific simulation engine. Thus the GRAMS reference model provides the necessary foundation to develop a model in such a way that it can be executed on various simulation engines.

The second requirement stated above addresses the technological trend towards multi-core processors. Treating current (and especially upcoming) multi-core processors like a distributed system will not result in optimal speedups. Multi-core processors and distributed systems are sufficiently different (e. g., regarding bandwidth and communication reliability between the cores respectively processors) to not just carry over well-known strategies for parallelization. Instead, to exploit the full potential of multi-core processors their specific characteristics have to be taken into account. The GRAMS reference model is independent of the implementation of different simulation engines which may exploit the underlying hardware in an optimal fashion. Therefore, the GRAMS reference model provides also the necessary foundation for fulfilling the second requirement.

3.3 Existing approaches and their limitations

Parallel simulation may either decompose the computation on a spatial basis or on a temporal basis [36, p. 177ff.]. Time-parallel simulation (i. e., a simulation using temporal decomposition) is highly sensitive to the state-matching problem [36, p. 178f.] and is considered hard to employ in case of complex state transitions [67]. As agent-based models are most often used to represent complex systems with various interactions between the agents, time-parallel simulation is not efficiently applicable to this kind of models.

This assumption is reinforced by the fact that agent-based models usually have a strong emphasis on the simulated environment (cp. Chapter 2.4). Lees et al. discuss the importance of the environment primarily with respect to distributed simulation and point out that the agents' environment resembles a large shared state of a multi-agent simulation. Therefore, 'the efficient simulation of the environment of a multi-agent simulation is perhaps the key problem in the distributed simulation' [76]. This statement is in accordance with findings of Logan and Theodoropoulos [127, 78, 128].

Various approaches for parallel multi-agent simulation have been proposed. Notably, all approaches known so far consider only spatial decomposition. Also, various simulation toolkits support parallel execution. A good overview of existing tools for parallel agent-based simulation is given by Pawlaszczyk [101, p. 126ff.]. In the following subsections, approaches most relevant in context of this thesis are described.

3.3.1 Pawlaszczyk (2009)

Pawlaszczyk [101] analyzes multi-agent simulations with regard to scalability and parallel execution of multi-agent simulations. The agent-based model is considered in traditional terms of parallel and distributed simulation: Each agent is treated as a separate logical process which in turn is executed by a separate thread [101, p. 165ff., p. 233]. Therefore, this work is concerned with parallel and distributed simulations in general, considering specific characteristics of agent-based models if possible.

Optimistic synchronization algorithms are devised which take into account agent-specific information. As communication between the agents is typical for agent-based models, synchronization methods are defined which exploit characteristics of the used communication protocol.

The devised algorithms are implemented using the Java Agent Development Framework (JADE) [5]. Within this framework each agent is realized as a separate thread. For comparison, three different thread synchronization mechanisms are implemented. Partitioning is static and has to be defined manually before starting a simulation.

Five test models have been used for experimentation. In total, up to 5 000 agents were simulated, utilizing up to 10 processors. The results indicate that the granularity of the events has a great impact on scalability. Furthermore, communication and interaction between the submodels (i. e., agents) severely limits scalability, especially if communication costs become larger compared to the actual computing time required for event processing.

Finally, Pawlaszczyk points out that the devised approach demonstrates for the first time that efficient simulation of agent-based models with up 5 000 agents is possible [101, p. 287, p. 279]. This statement seems exaggerated as successful agent-based simulations with up to

300 million agents are reported [97]. He concludes by assuming that a large class of agent-based models is scalable if the models possess inherent parallelism and computation costs outweigh communication costs.

3.3.2 Logan, Theodoropoulos (2001)

Logan and Theodoropoulos developed the notion of *Spheres of Influence* for distributed simulation of multi-agent systems [78, 127, 75]. A *sphere of influence* defines the spatial area within the simulated environment which is potentially affected by an agents action. For each action, the sphere of influence is limited to the immediate consequences. The spheres of influences may then be used to spatially decompose the model into independent components.

The computation of disjoint subsets of interacting agents is envisaged to be updated dynamically. This way, dynamic behavior of the model may be utilized and partitioning potentially improved. The basic idea is to partition the model in a way that interactions between partitions are minimized. The primary measure for deciding whether a partition of the model should be divided further is the pattern and frequency of state accesses.

Based on preliminary results, Logan and Theodorpoulos conclude that the proposed framework may be feasible but that further work is required to establish a general applicability [78]. Unfortunately, no reports on further work could be found.

3.3.3 P. Riley, G. Riley (2003)

P. Riley and G. Riley present an approach for distributed simulation of software-in-the-loop agents [110, 109]. The simulation environment outlined is specifically designed to interoperate with a wide variety of agents. Basically the simulation environment provides the framework into which different agents may be integrated. All agents have to connect to a central master process. This master process is responsible for managing the central event list (containing all events scheduled by the agents) as well as managing the world model (i. e., the simulated environment).

In contrast to other approaches, the proposed system provides only support for the distribution of the agents themselves. Distribution of the world model is not directly supported. Furthermore, automatic distribution of agents according to some specific performance measure is not addressed. Also, the problem of multiple agents trying to alter the same portion of the world model is not considered explicitly.

3.3.4 Scheutz, Schermerhorn (2006)

Similarly to the *spheres of influence*-approach, Scheutz and Schermerhorn describe the parallel execution of an agent-based model based on the notion of *update independence* [114]. Actions of two agents are considered to be update-independent if the state changes induced by these actions do not influence each other. Of course, update-independent actions can be executed in parallel. In order to compute update-independent sets, Scheutz and Schermerhorn propose to utilize sensor and actuator ranges of agents. The range possibly affected by an agent's action is denoted as *event horizon*. Whereas the spheres of influence denote an area actually affected by an action, the event horizon represents an area possibly affected by an action.

Scheutz and Schermerhorn have proven that parallel execution of their algorithm produces identical results as sequential execution. Experimental validation shows almost linear scaling with the number of employed processors in well-chosen scenarios. Without the need to evaluate whether actions are in conflict with each other, the computational cost associated with the agents behavior and corresponding state changes is identified as dominant factor [114].

The crucial aspect of this approach is having 'an efficient way to detect update independence' [114]. Although it is proposed to utilize the sensor and actuator ranges it remains unclear whether computing update independent sets is possible in less than quadratic complexity. Furthermore, the results indicate severe weaknesses of this approach

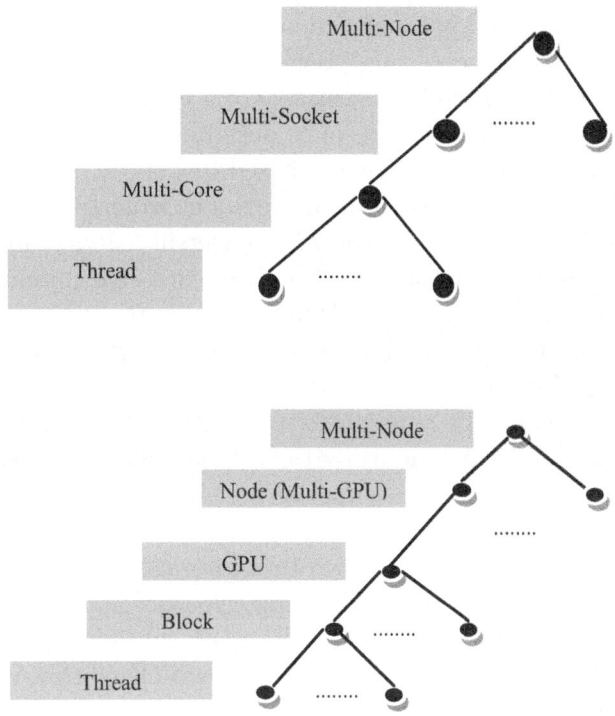

Figure 3.2: Illustration of multi-platform computing hierarchies [6].

when moving from well-chosen scenarios to more complex and less well-ordered setups.

3.3.5 Aaby et al. (2010)

A recent approach of Aaby et al. [6] discusses parallelization of agent-based simulations on multi-platform hierarchies. As illustrated in Figure 3.2 the computation hierarchy may include multi-core processors and multi-node systems as well as graphical processing units (GPU). The approach explicitly addresses the issue of exploiting current hardware, especially multi-core processors and high-performance graphics processors.

In contrast to the approaches described before, the approach described in [6] considers a very specific class of agent-based models. Namely, agent-based models consisting of a grid of blocks containing the agents. Dependencies are only possible in neighboring blocks. This rather simplistic type of agent-based model restricts the number of possible applications which is also evident from the presented examples. Both examples (Game of Life, Leadership Model) are basically based on a cellular automaton. To reduce excessive communication, neighboring partitions overlap. Due to the nature of the underlying cellular automata, an overlap of n cells requires synchronization only once every n time steps.

On the one hand, the approach is very interesting as various different hardware platforms are utilized in a hierarchical manner. On the other hand, the underlying assumption of cellular automata is a severe restriction with respect to common use cases of agent-based modeling and simulation. Firstly, very often interaction and dependency relations are not limited to neighboring cells. Secondly, explicit interference of actions (i. e., conflicting actions) is not addressed. Thirdly, the assumption of a time-stepped execution with fixed time increments is in contrast to event-driven simulations.

3.3.6 Further related work

In [134] Uhrmacher and Gugler present a test bed for deliberative agents which supports parallel execution of agents. Rooted in the domain of developing multi-agent systems, one major issue was to take into account the deliberation time of each agent adequately. Like most test beds the deliberation time is based on the actually consumed computing time. The simulation environment used (JAMES) employs a parallel DEVS approach. The distributed execution was evaluated using a Tileworld scenario with at most two agents. In conclusion, their algorithm executes multiple agents in an execution time comparable to the time required for simulating a single agent (given a sufficient number of computers).

A highly scalable agent-based model for simulating the spreading of diseases is presented in [97]. As the author points out, the most immediate problem is that the size of the population (in this case approximately 300 million agents) exceeds the memory of a single computer. Distribution of the agents is therefore driven by the constrained resources of a single computer (especially memory limitations). The devised load-balancing approach tries to weigh the influence of smaller agent subsets using a larger number of computers versus the increased communication overhead introduced with each new agent subset. In this special case, minimizing inter-node communication is the way to achieving highest speedups. However, the results presented make use of only two nodes, each of them executing eight threads.

Regarding existing multi-agent toolkits, various attempts have been made regarding distributed multi-agent simulation. Distributed execution based on the Java Agent Development Framework (JADE) is discussed in [86]. As JADE is primarily designed to be a framework for multi-agent systems, it lacks several features usually regarded essential for multi-agent simulation (e. g., proper time management). Furthermore, frameworks originating from the domain of multi-agent systems are usually designed to execute a small number of agents. The major findings presented in [86] are that inter-agent communication may cause substantial delays and that (depending on the number of agents) local or global synchronization should be preferred. Reducing communication as well as redistributing agents is considered for improving the performance.

Similarly, Gianni et al. propose DisSimJADE as a distributed simulation framework on top of JADE [44]. Following the layered SimArch architecture [43], DisSimJADE allows transparent execution either in a local or distributed environment. A brief example scenario is provided, using a graph-based environment to represent a manufacturing system. Actual results and experiences are not reported in [44].

A distributed discrete-event simulation engine that explicitly highlights the isolation of the modeling domain from the simulation engine is described in [104]. Separating these two aspects is stressed as an important element of this approach. This property is emphasized by the existence of eight different simulation engines which produce 'in (almost) all cases' [104] identical simulation results. Unfortunately, detailed performance benchmarks or results from practical applications are missing. A separation of model, abstract simulator and actual simulation algorithm is also stressed by [94].

Rogers and Harless treat discrete-event simulation applied to the simulation of autonomous agents on a more theoretical level [111]. After discussing the benefits and drawbacks of different simulation world views (event scheduling, activity scanning, process interaction), they address the fundamental question how to partition a model. As they point out, complex scenarios will most likely always involve a non-uniform distribution of agents. They conclude that static partitioning methods may not be well-suited as the distribution of agents may change over time and that 'collision events remain the central classification for events of interest' [111].

Long et al. analyzed the influence of static agent distribution compared to dynamic agent distribution taking into account additional information like communication relations [79]. One major finding is that performance improvements due to dynamic agent distribution are observed, although the improvement is much more significant when larger number of agents are simulated (more than 1 000 agents). This leads to the conclusion that for small numbers of agents static random agent distribution strategies may be sufficient.

4 Summary

Complex systems are characterized by multiple entities, often of heterogeneous nature, that are interacting in many ways. The causes of complexity are manifold: relationships and dependencies of system components, number and value range of model parameters, or intricate behavior and interaction patterns of single entities may cause complexity. Agent-based modeling is a modeling paradigm which is well suited for representing such complex systems. The main benefit of agent-based models is a close structural similarity of a system under investigation and a corresponding simulation model.

Although a certain common understanding of agent-based modeling exists, there is no exhaustive and generally accepted specification defining what actually comprises an agent-based model. Several research approaches exist which try to give such a definition of agent-based modeling. Unfortunately, all approaches known so far are suffering from various weaknesses. In summary, a well-specified definition of agent-based modeling including a development framework is missing.

Existing approaches considering parallel execution of multi-agent simulations always focus on a specific domain. Furthermore, existing approaches are often developed with specific decomposition patterns in mind. Generally applicable partitioning strategies or approaches for parallel execution of agent-based models and simulations are hardly available. Existing approaches are not only application dependent, but – as simulation models and simulation engines are often not strictly separated – the approaches for partitioning simulation models are also tightly integrated into the simulation engines. The result is that simulation models, simulation engines and parallelization approaches are highly interwoven and hardly distinguishable in currently reported work. Static as well as dynamic parallelization approaches are proposed, yet reported applications are rare and benchmarks are only available for very few and specific use cases.

Part II

Effective and efficient model development

5 The need for a reference model for agent-based modeling and simulation

This chapter highlights why a reference model for agent-based modeling and simulation is needed. Current problems and needs concerning design, development and application of agent-based modeling and simulation are presented first. Afterwards, terminology and purpose of reference models are presented, followed by requirements for a reference model for agent-based modeling and simulation.

5.1 Current problems and needs of agent-based modeling and simulation

Building upon related work presented in chapters 2.3 and 2.4, the following sections summarize current problems and needs in the area of agent-based modeling and simulation.

5.1.1 Weak definitions of basic terms and concepts

Although currently in widespread use, the foundations of agent-based modeling and simulation appear to be a lot weaker compared to alternative modeling paradigms [69]. Surprisingly, this includes ambiguous definitions of basic terms (e. g., which elements comprise an agent-based model and how are they related to each other) as well as missing definitions of advanced concepts (e. g., what is to be understood exactly by the simulation of an agent-based model) [91, 60].

Various approaches and formal models have been developed and proposed in the past (see Chapter 2.3). Each approach usually focusses on some specific objective and therefore often trades generally accepted principles and ideas for the advancement in this specific area (e. g., unclear distinction between a model and its simulation). Furthermore, existing approaches of suitable generality often simplify key aspects in an unacceptable way (e. g., actions without duration). Accordingly, more precise definitions of key notions and concepts of agent-based modeling as a prerequisite to establish a common understanding are necessary [60, 91, 13, 46].

Resulting from unclear key notions and imprecisely defined basic concepts of agent-based modeling, the *simulation* of agent-based models is often equally weak defined. This unsatisfactory state was summarized by Müller who observed that 'most, if not all, existing multi-agent simulation platforms produce simulation results which do not depend only on the model but on the way the model is implemented and the scheduling ordered, this ordering being at worst arbitrary and at best randomized' [89], see also [101, p. 148].

The lack of a well-defined foundation as a basis for developing specific simulation engines is acknowledged independently by Wagner and Himmelspach. Wagner observed that many agent-based simulation systems do not have a theoretical foundation and advocates a simulation metamodel as well as an abstract simulator architecture and execution model [139, 137]. Himmelspach recalls that a lot of simulation systems were developed in past years and almost all of them focus on some specific formalism, language and execution paradigm (e. g., sequential, distributed). In this context, Himmelspach observes that repeated re-development is very time-consuming and usually distracts from the intended investigations. This disadvantage becomes even more obvious against the background of the (admittedly subjective) statement of Minar that 'unfortunately, computer modeling frequently turns good scientists into bad programmers' [88].

5.1.2 Bad support of collaborative development

Assuming that simulation models grow in size and complexity, it seems likely that future model development will require large teams of different specialists working together. Talking about large and complex models, both in concept and software, the importance of sound and precise definitions becomes even more obvious if these models are developed by a large number of people.

A reference model for agent-based modeling and simulation could be very helpful in at least two aspects: First, it would provide necessary basic definitions in an unambiguous way. Thereby the reference model would provide a common understanding shared by all project members, simplifying communication and reducing the risk of misunderstandings. As this kind of common understanding is crucial for the success of projects as they reach a certain complexity, a common (and accepted) reference model may result in considerable benefits.

Second, such a reference model can be regarded as a linking element between all project members. This is especially important for bringing together specialists from different fields (e. g., modeling and implementation) on the one hand and decoupling the responsibilities and work areas of the specialists on the other hand. Here, decoupling of responsibilities refers to the fact that the reference model allows the identification of independent parts which may in turn be given to mostly independently operating teams. In this case, the reference model can be seen as a kind of interface specification, detailing precisely how the various pieces fit together.

Furthermore, the reference model might simplify development and usage of platforms for coordinating collaborative development. As collaboration requires all project members to have access to the latest information and data of a model, enabling such supportive platforms is important.

5.1.3 Need for improvement of quality by standardization

Agent-based models as well as simulation engines are often custom-made and tailored for one specific application. This is fine for models, but unnecessary for simulation engines. As modeling and simulation should strive from art towards an engineering approach, it is obvious that a general approach for describing agent-based models and their simulation is still missing. Furthermore, 'the use of standardized scientific apparatus is not only a convenience: it allows one to *divide through* by the common equipment, thereby aiding the production of repeatable, comparable research results' [88]. The envisioned reference model might close this gap and is a step towards some kind of standardization.

5.2 General purpose of reference models

According to [115] reference models are development guidelines providing standardized solutions for certain modeling problems of a (homogeneous) class of real systems. Although many definitions are along these lines, Thomas points out that a clear and common definition of the term *reference model* is missing [130, 129]. Reference models are usually characterized by the two main attributes *universality* and *recommendation character* [130, 129].

Universality refers to the idea that a reference model should be applicable not only in one special case but to a certain class of problems. This characteristic can be found in various definitions (cp. [129, p. 21ff.]), yet due to the fact that a reference model is valid only within certain boundaries, Thomas denotes this characteristic as 'inexpedient' [130].

Recommendation character refers to the idea that a reference model should serve as a blueprint or even as a default solution for certain modeling problems. Like universality, recommendation character is also subject to discussion, as 'for example, it is unclear how the quality of a recommendation for a reference model can be verified' [130].

A very simplistic and pragmatic definition for reference models is given by Modi et al.: 'Any generic model that has specific examples can be considered to be a reference model' [91]. They continue by stating that reference models provide patterns for solving specific problems instead of prescribing how functions and systems should be implemented. According to Modi et al. the purpose of reference models is 'to enable others to practice their discipline with a solid foundation' [91]. Within this thesis the term *reference model* is defined according to Thomas [130, 129]:

Definition 11 (Reference model) A *reference model* is a model used for supporting the construction of other models. □

Sometimes the term *meta model* is used synonymously. Within this thesis only the term *reference model* is used.

Reference models have a lot in common with standardization activities. They create a common understanding of terms and concepts, help to clarify (or even define) the semantics of systems and increase comparability among models defined or documented this way. The applicability of a reference model is determined by the number of problems for which it may be used [115]. Of course, universality of a reference model depends crucially on the degrees of freedom a model developer has for adapting a reference model to problem-specific needs. Common major aims for using reference models are to reduce the complexity of a modeling task at hand and to simplify development processes. In general, a reduction of efforts in time and cost is expected, although well-founded field reports are not available.

5.3 Requirements for a reference model

Based on the survey of existing approaches for specifying agent-based models and their simulation (see Chapter 2.3) and the goals of this thesis, this section summarizes the main requirements for a reference model for agent-based modeling and simulation.

5.3.1 Clear distinction between model and simulation engine

A reference model should strictly separate between a simulation model and a simulation engine that executes a model. This reduces the complexity significantly and provides the necessary basis for future work on collaborative development and distributed execution of agent-based models. As this separation is a key requirement, it will be explained in more detail.

First of all, such a reference model should focus on the conceptual (and partly the formal) model development. Given this intention, on the highest level

- the agent-based simulation model itself,

- the execution (simulation) of this model and

- the simulation engines used for execution

are distinguished.

The *agent-based simulation model* describes the entities (e. g., agents and objects) as well as interactions of these entities in a common environment. Building upon the agent-based model, the *execution* (simulation) of a model is defined. This includes especially the behavior of possibly conflicting agents (including conflict detection and resolution).

The *simulation engines* should not be directly part of a reference model, as a multitude of simulation engines can be thought of. Any simulation engine may be used as long as it complies with the reference model.

Separating these aspects and thereby reducing the complexity is a necessary precondition for a clear definition of basic notions and key concepts of agent-based modeling and simulation. Furthermore, a strict separation of these different aspects allows a high decomposability and by providing well-defined interfaces an efficient modeling process on the one hand and a flexible way of execution on the other hand.

At this point, it should be mentioned that DEVS strictly distinguishes between model and simulator [151], and that extensions of original DEVS specifically address agent-based modeling [131].

5.3.2 Simulated environment

Given the importance many authors ascribe to the modeling of the simulated environment, these remarks have to be taken into account [52, 146, 76, 70]. The environment is seen as a mostly passive background providing the common playground for the agents. Nevertheless, the environment may possess its own processes which may alter its state (e. g., some kind of diffusion processes) and may therefore generate events which can be perceived by agents. In this context it is important to mention that agents have to perceive their environment explicitly and that this perception (depending on model purpose and an agents sensors) can be erroneous (cp. *internal model* in [132, 131]).

Due to the variety of areas where agent-based models are employed, a reference model has to support different types of environments. Although mostly spatial environments (e. g., 2-dimensional or 3-dimensional) are used, other types of environments must be possible (e. g., graph-like environments).

5.3.3 Simulation time

The simulation time has to be modeled explicitly and completely independent, i. e., without restrictions to issues like execution paradigm (time-stepped, event-driven, etc.). Simulation engines may be implemented rather arbitrary as long as they are conforming to the specified reference model.

Explicit modeling of simulation time is hardly new to anyone familiar with modeling and simulation. It is nevertheless mentioned explicitly due to many limitations currently often present in agent-based models and simulations (like time-stepped execution with fixed time increments, see Section 2.3.7). Another reason is that the terms

Multi-Agent-*Simulation* and Multi-Agent-*System* are often confused
or at least used synonymously without much care. As time models are
quite a new challenge in the context of Multi-Agent-Systems (cp. [51])
one might easily mix things up.

5.3.4 Agents and objects

A reference model has to support at least two different types of entities:
agents and objects. The term *agent* refers to an entity with some
kind of autonomous and pro-active behavior (cp. [35, p. 308]). The
term *object* refers to entities within the agent-based model that do
not exhibit any pro-active behavior, i. e., to entities that are passive
but may, of course, be altered by agents (e. g., items or resources).
Objects are situated within an environment and therefore it is the
choice of a model developer whether a specific part of a model is
represented as object or environment. A good indicator for modeling
parts as an object is the amount of interaction expected with this part.
If the degree of interaction is high, modeling such parts as individual
objects is often beneficial (e. g., picking up items and carrying them
around).

With reference to [35, p. 308], it seems appropriate to point out
that *objects* in the sense of this reference model are not necessarily
related to objects known from object-oriented programming or other
object-based systems. Although it is of course possible to implement
agents and (model) objects using object-oriented languages, in this
thesis the term *object* refers to objects as part of the agent-based
model.

5.3.5 Actions, effects and constraints

Actions of agents have a duration and can interfere with each other.
In combination with an explicit time model this imposes especially
that different actions can have different durations. There should be no
need that durations of actions are a multiple of some smallest possible
time step.

It is stressed that agents can only control their effectors but not necessarily the outcome of their actions (cp. Section 2.3.7). Therefore, agents have to determine which effector they want to use, but a simulation engine has to take care of the computation of the actual outcome and possible effects. In order for actions to fail (i. e., produce effects different from the intended ones) decision rules are necessary. These rules are defined within a simulation model and enforced by a simulation engine. As they limit the autonomy of agents they are also denoted as *laws* or *constraints* [14, 116].

5.3.6 Abstraction from specific agent architectures

The internal structure of agents and their behavior model are not of primary interest in context of this thesis. Nevertheless, as 'nearly all systems ... constitute a definite intra-agent architecture' [24] a reference model must be able to represent different agent architectures.

This requirement is in agreement with assumptions made by Modi et al. for the agent layer of the Agent Systems Reference Model: 'We make no assumptions about the internal processing structures of an agent. An agent could be built with a complex cognitive model or it could be a simple rulebased system' [91].

5.3.7 Formal specification

The development of a reference model for agent-based modeling and simulation that is precise in its definitions as well as unambiguous in its interpretation requires, in general, a formal or semi-formal specification. Besides guaranteeing the exactness of definitions, a formal specification could also provide the necessary well-defined basis for the intended future use and investigations. On the other hand, a reference model has to be flexible, adoptable to actual problems and (more or less) easily comprehensible.

Therefore, these two contrasting requirements need to be balanced. Although precision and clarity are predominant requirements, it is also important that a formal specification is flexible enough to cope with the various requirements of describing actual agent-based models. Furthermore, a formal specification should not impose unnecessary limitations or hurdles (cp. [69]). A current overview of formal specification approaches is given in [11].

Within the M&S-community, a number of modeling formalisms are available, like e. g., process calculi, timed automata, DEVS or (labelled) transition systems. Currently, widely accepted standards for describing reference models are not available but an open research topic [34, p. 13ff.].

As important as the intended purpose of a formalization is to know the activities which the chosen formalism has to support. Therefore, a second reason for formalizing a reference model would be the intention to support some kind of formal verification or automatic processing (e. g., reasoning, inferencing). Also, direct transformation of a formal specification into executable code is of interest. However, currently no such activities are intended.

With reference to the intended purpose and an addressed modeling level of (primarily) the conceptual model, a formal specification is not considered a must-have requirement in this thesis. This does, of course, not imply that a reference model is allowed to be inaccurate or ambiguous. On the contrary: a reference model should strive for maximum clarity and exactness. Therefore, parts of a reference model may be formalized (where appropriate) using a formalism suitable for this purpose.

Furthermore, a reference model may provide suggestions which parts of a problem-specific model should be formalized and which formalisms might be suitable. Future revisions of a reference model should built upon first experiences gained with the current reference model and strive for a more formal specification.

6 GRAMS – General Reference Model for Agent-based Modeling and Simulation

Based upon the requirements specified in the previous chapter, this chapter presents the *General Reference Model for Agent-based Modeling and Simulation* (GRAMS).

6.1 Aims and target audience

The *General Reference Model for Agent-based Modeling and Simulation* (GRAMS), as proposed in the following, aims to

- identify key notions and concepts of agent-based models and their relations,

- provide precise definitions of key concepts of agent-based models and their simulation,

- provide a general template for specification and documentation of agent-based models,

- provide an abstract basis for development of simulation engines used for simulating agent-based models.

A reference model with precise definitions provides the basis for a common understanding which in turn may improve model development, testing and reusability. The primary intention of the reference model is not to specify technical recommendations, but to provide a conceptual framework for agent-based modeling and simulation.

In order to provide a conceptual framework that is general enough for a wide range of applications, a reasonable abstraction level has to be chosen. The guiding principle which is followed throughout the reference model is to avoid prescriptive requirements as far as possible and make these only when necessary. A central design principle is abstraction of specific agent architectures (i.e., of specific internal structures and behavior modeling of agents) as well as abstraction from specific simulation engines.

The target audience of this reference model are model developers and scientist in the area of agent-based modeling and simulation. The reference model can help and guide model developers in creating and documenting agent-based models in a well-defined way, thereby providing a common language and understanding. Application developers may build upon this reference model to create simulation engines which adhere to common specifications and allow execution of agent-based models on various simulation engines. The scientific community may use the reference model to develop and describe concepts and algorithms on a higher level, thereby gaining advantage of more general results which are applicable in a wider range than before.

6.2 Basic idea of the GRAMS reference model

Figure 6.1 illustrates the basic idea of the GRAMS reference model. Firstly, the GRAMS reference model defines basic building blocks of agent-based models in a domain-independent way and serves as a template for problem-specific instantiations, defining generic components, their interrelations as well as their semantics. Therefore, each simulation model representing some system under investigation needs to be instantiated as a problem-specific model.

Secondly, the GRAMS reference model defines constraints for the simulation of an agent-based model. The definition of constraints for the simulation of an agent-based model provides the starting point for implementing different simulation engines. A simulation

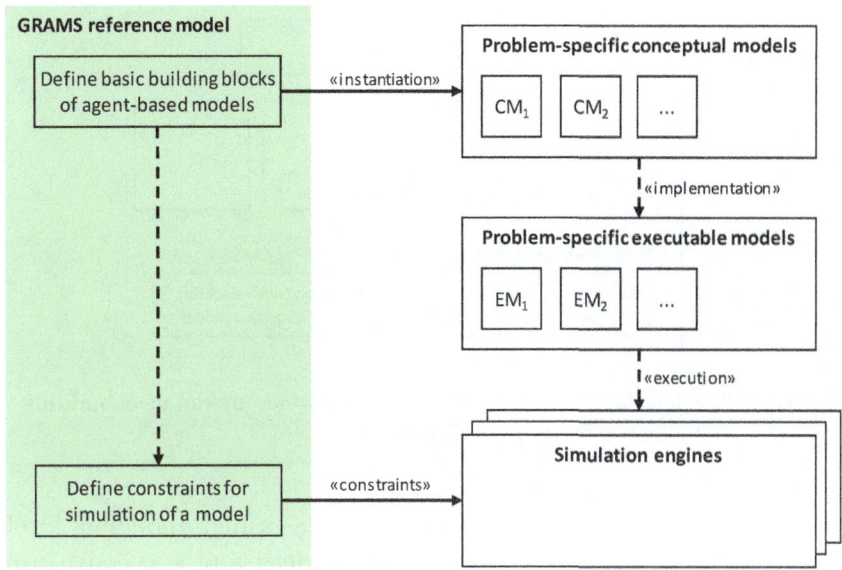

Figure 6.1: The GRAMS reference model serves as a template for problem-specific conceptual models and defines constraints on simulation engines for executing these models.

engine may use any kind of internal data structures and execution control as long as the constraints specified by the GRAMS reference model are not violated. The important point is that all simulation engines produce identical results when executing the same model under identical conditions (like same random seed, etc.). By providing precise definitions the GRAMS reference model allows to develop simulation models and simulation engines independently of each other.

As expectations on such a *general* reference model for agent-based modeling and simulation vary a lot, it is important to place the GRAMS reference model into proper context. Figure 6.2 classifies the domain of agent-based modeling along the *modeling level.* This is a rather soft indicator ranging from low-level modeling to more and more sophisticated high-level modeling approaches. Low-level modeling considers only basic ideas and concepts, and represents

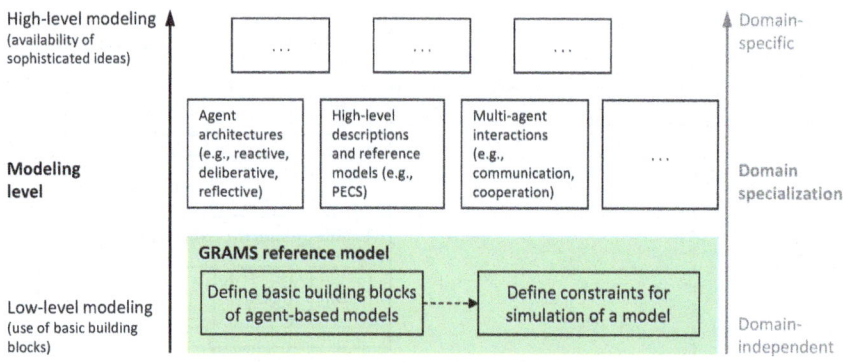

Figure 6.2: Classification of the GRAMS reference model as a building block for further development.

modeling on a very elementary level, whereas a high modeling level is connected to the use of sophisticated ideas and successive use of concepts from lower levels. As indicated in Figure 6.2, a higher modeling level is often a synonym for a stronger domain specialization.

In providing definitions of the basic ideas and concepts of agent-based modeling, the GRAMS reference model is classified as a *low level* and *domain-independent* approach.

6.3 Definition of an agent-based model

An agent-based model M is defined as tuple $M = (\mathbb{T}, \mathbb{E}, \mathbb{ENT}, emb, \mathbb{EV}, \mathbb{C})$ with

$\mathbb{T}$	set of points in time,
$\mathbb{E} = (\mathbb{L}, \mathbb{P}, \mathbb{U})$	environment, consisting of a set of locations $\mathbb{L}$, environmental properties $\mathbb{P}$ and update functions $\mathbb{U}$,
$\mathbb{ENT}$	set of entities,
$emb : \mathbb{ENT} \to \mathbb{L}$	embedding of entities in the environment,
$\mathbb{EV}$	set of event types,
$\mathbb{C}$	set of constraints.

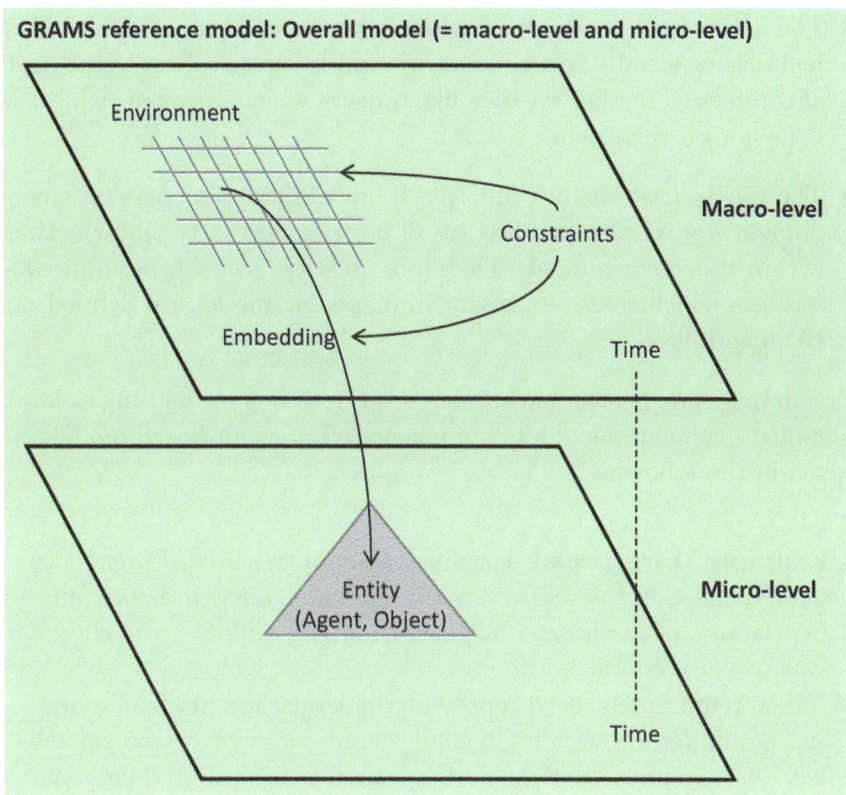

Figure 6.3: Macro- and micro-level of the GRAMS reference model.

As a model is subject to change, the state S of a model M at a specific point in time $t \in \mathbb{T}$ is defined as $S_t(M) = (S_t(\mathbb{E}), \mathbb{ENT}_t, emb_t)$.

The GRAMS reference model defines single agents as well as the simulation of a model containing multiple agents, thus the GRAMS reference model applies to the micro-level as well as to the macro-level of an agent-based model. The interrelation between those two levels of modeling is illustrated in Figure 6.3 and with respect to the GRAMS reference model the following distinction is adopted:

- The *micro-level* is concerned with properties of a single entity. This includes especially inner structure and behavior of an agent, but also refers to further entities like objects which may not exhibit a behavior on their own.

- The *macro-level* defines the overall model, i. e., the common environment and the embedding of all entities currently (inter)acting within this environment. Therefore, possible event types and constraints which may be present in a specific model are defined on the macro-level.

Simulation time has to be considered on both macro- and micro-level. Detailed explanations of all components of an agent-based model are given in the following.

Example: Firespread For illustration of the GRAMS reference model, the example of a fireman fighting against fire spreading in a landscape is chosen. Inspired from [58] and [89], the chosen scenario also contains a firebug.

The requirement is to represent the landscape made of empty spaces and forests with its dynamics of fire occurrence and spreading. It is assumed that the firebug wanders around randomly and ignites some forest with a given (low) probability. As long as no fire is detected, the fireman is waiting at his current position. If a fire occurs, he moves towards the fire. When on a burning place, he waters the surface. The model uses an environment composed of cells with a Moore topology (i. e., each cell has 8 neighbors). Each cell can be either empty, with forest, watered, burning or burned (see Figure 6.4). A cell with forest may be ignited by the firebug; a fireman is positioned on the cells with the objective to stop the fire(s).   ◁

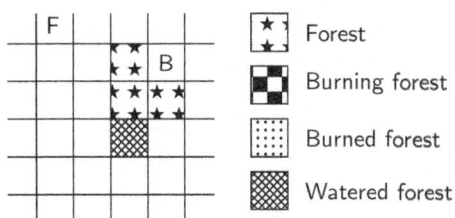

Figure 6.4: The example scenario uses a 2-dimensional environment with five different cell types (empty, forest, burning, burned, watered). Two agents are present: a fireman (F) and a firebug (B).

6.4 Macro-level modeling

The macro-level of the GRAMS reference model deals with all aspects concerning integration of entities into a common environment and interaction of multiple entities.

6.4.1 Simulation time

The *simulation time* $\mathbb{T}$ is defined as totally ordered set of points in time (i. e., antisymmetry, transitivity and totality are fulfilled), cp. [151, p. 99f.], [36, p. 28]. The definition of simulation time in this generality imposes the least constraints on the further modeling of agent behavior and event handling.

Depending on the actual application, simulation time may be defined in a *bottom-up* fashion, first defining simulation time on the micro-level and subsequently deriving the simulation time on the macro-level as a superset of all locally used simulation times. This allows developers of different parts of a simulation model (e. g., different kinds of agents) to use simulation times which are best-suited in their specific case.

The opposite approach is to define simulation time in *top-down* manner. In this case, simulation time is defined on the macro-level first, and all entities on the micro-level have to use a subset of this simulation time. The strict compliance of simulation time used on the micro- and macro-level has to be ensured in any case. Both approaches, bottom-up and top-down, may also be applied to the development of the whole agent-based model.

It should be pointed out that the GRAMS reference model does not imply the use of discrete time. At least within the conceptual model a continuous time may be specified if suited for the model purpose. Of course, a discretization of simulation time is usually unavoidable in the course of the implementation as an executable software.

Example: Firespread A discrete simulation time is chosen, i. e., $\mathbb{T} = \mathbb{N}$. For this example, a single time step represents an interval of 1 minute.   ◁

6.4.2 Environment

In order to define actions of single agents and interactions between multiple simulated agents, the common environment needs to be defined. As an abstraction of the real environment, the *environment* $\mathbb{E}$ denotes the common space in which all agents are acting. As for the simulation time, restrictions imposed by the GRAMS reference model are quite low: the simulated environment may be discrete or continuous, bounded or unbounded and can be of arbitrary dimension (although often 2-dimensional or 3-dimensional environments are used). Except for environmental dynamics the environment is assumed to be passive, but of course changeable.

Definition 12 (Environment) The environment $\mathbb{E} = (\mathbb{L}, \mathbb{P}, \mathbb{U})$ is defined as tuple of locations $\mathbb{L}$, environmental properties $\mathbb{P}$ and environmental update functions $\mathbb{U}$.   □

In order to embed entities into the environment at specific places, the concept of *locations* is introduced. A location $l \in \mathbb{L}$ simply denotes some connected space within the environment, with $\mathbb{L}$ denoting the set of all possible locations. As the set of locations may change (e. g., due to an expanding world) $S_t(\mathbb{L})$ denotes the set of locations at time *t*. Although this may often not be necessary, this definition keeps the possibility open.

As agent-based models are often used for representing complex systems, interactions between entities are a very important aspect. As entities (agents as well as objects) are situated within the environment, actions of agents as well as interactions are often also influenced by the environment. Therefore, it is often required, to define a metric on the environment which is a function m defining the distance between two points: $m : \mathbb{L} \times \mathbb{L} \to \mathbb{R}$. As a metric is not always necessary, the GRAMS reference model does not require its definition.

The set $\mathbb{P} = \{p_i\}$ denotes *environmental properties* (e. g., temperature, humidity, gravitation) which are associated with specific locations:

$$p_i : \mathbb{L} \to \mathcal{D}_i \qquad (6.1)$$

$\mathcal{D}_i$ denotes the actual domain of the property p_i. For example, temperature might be modeled by discrete values in degrees Celsius, while humidity may be represented by continuous values in percent. The actual value of all properties at time t is denoted by $S_t(\mathbb{P})$.

To model environmental dynamics properties of each location may be altered by *environmental update functions* $u_i \in \mathbb{U}$:

$$u_i : \mathbb{L} \times \mathbb{P} \to \mathbb{P} \qquad (6.2)$$

As defined later on, update functions are triggered by events and may trigger new events themselves. Each update function has a duration which represents the time interval from triggering until the actual state change. An update function may also trigger itself again. $S_t(\mathbb{U})$ denotes the state of all update functions at a point in time t.

As the environment may change over time, the state of the environment is always only defined for a specific point in time:

Definition 13 (State of the environment) The state S of the environment $\mathbb{E}$ at a point in time t is $S_t(\mathbb{E}) = (S_t(\mathbb{L}), S_t(\mathbb{P}), S_t(\mathbb{U}))$. $\quad\square$

Example: Firespread The environment is modeled as a rectangular grid of $n_x \times n_y$ cells:

$$\mathbb{L} = \{ \quad (1,1), \quad (2,1), \quad \ldots, \quad (n_x, 1),$$
$$(1,2), \quad (2,2), \quad \ldots, \quad (n_x, 2),$$
$$\vdots \qquad \vdots \qquad \ddots \qquad \vdots \qquad \qquad (6.3)$$
$$(1, n_y), \quad (2, n_y), \quad \ldots, \quad (n_x, n_y) \quad \}$$

A cell can be of five different types (empty, forest, burning, burned, watered) and each cell has a property p_{trees} denoting how many living trees are on this cell:

$$\mathbb{P} = \{ \quad p_{\text{type}} : \mathbb{L} \to \{empty, forest, burning, burned, watered\},$$
$$p_{\text{trees}} : \mathbb{L} \to \mathbb{N} \qquad \qquad \qquad \qquad \qquad \qquad \}$$
$$(6.4)$$

The update function u_{burn} decreases p_{trees} by one in each time step as long as the current cell has living trees:

$$\mathbb{U} = \{u_{\text{burn}} : \mathbb{L} \times p_{\text{trees}} \to p_{\text{trees}}\} \qquad (6.5)$$

with $l \in \mathbb{L}$:

$$u_{\text{burn}}(l, p_{\text{trees}}) = \begin{cases} p_{\text{trees}}(l) - 1 & \text{if } p_{\text{trees}}(l) > 0 \\ p_{\text{trees}}(l) & \text{if } p_{\text{trees}}(l) \leq 0 \end{cases}$$

◁

6.4.3 Embedding of entities

Given the set ENT_t of entities (consisting of agents and objects, see Section 6.6) at some specific point in time and the set of locations $S_t(\mathbb{L})$, the embedding of entities in the environment is defined straightforward:

$$emb_t : \text{ENT}_t \to S_t(\mathbb{L}) \qquad (6.6)$$

This definition associates each entity with a specific location within the environment. Two important aspects should be noted:

1. The embedding imposes no restrictions whether a location may be occupied by a limited number of entities only.

2. On the macro-level, inner structure and state of entities is not of interest. The embedding defines the current position of any entity at any specific point in time, i.e., *emb* defines the *ground truth* (i.e., undistorted information) as opposed to *perceived truth* (i.e., the position assumed by an agent) which may differ [122].

6.5 Events

Events are an integral part of any agent-based model and are also an essential part of the GRAMS reference model.

Definition 14 (Event) An *event* e is defined as an instantaneous occurrence at a specific point in time $t_e \in \mathbb{T}$ that may change the state of the model [16, p. 11]. □

Events are timeless which means that all events are *consumed* in the same moment they occur. Multiple events may occur at the same point in time, furthermore all events are distinguishable and can be associated with specific properties (e.g., type of event, area of influence).

The events defined by the GRAMS reference model may trigger actions of agents, which in turn may change the model state. A specific implementation of a simulation engine may represent such actions by a start-event and an end-event. Therefore, it is important to distinguish between the GRAMS reference model (defining events and actions on the level of the conceptual model) and a technical realization (executable model). With regard to technical realization, a specific implementation of a simulation engine may be event-driven. On the other hand, a simulation engine does not need to be event-driven and can as well use a time-stepped execution, as long as all specifications of the GRAMS reference model are fulfilled.

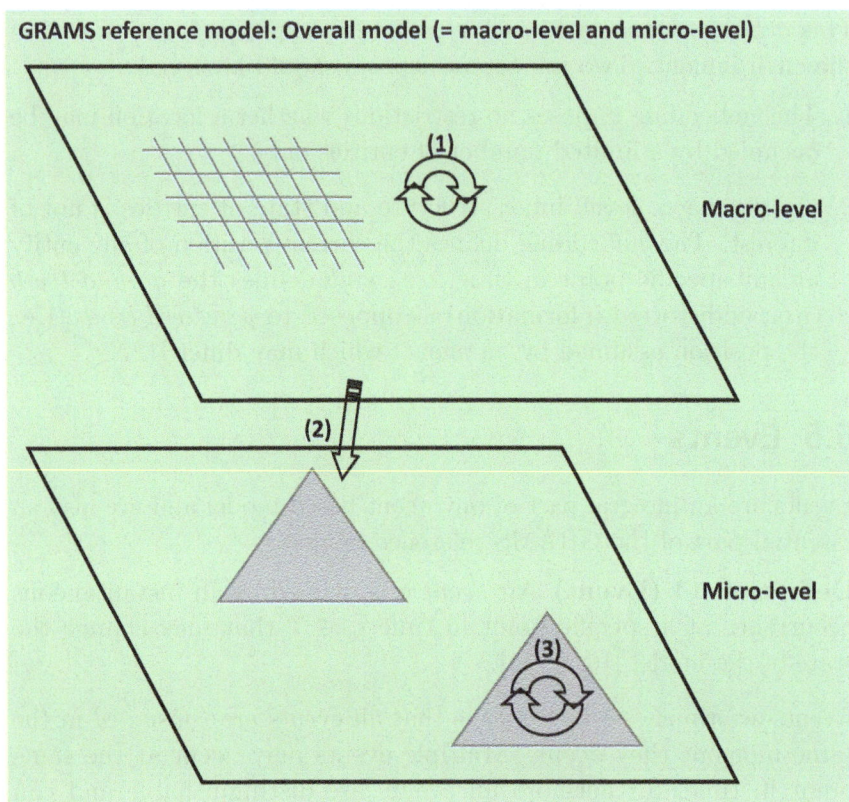

Figure 6.5: Illustration of event categories defined by the GRAMS reference model.

Two disjoint sets of events are distinguished: *Endogenous* events are occurring within a specific agent or within the environment and affect only the agent respectively the environment. *Exogenous* events on the other hand describe events occuring in one component of a model and affecting another component [16, p. 11].

Figure 6.5 illustrates the resulting event categories defined by the GRAMS reference model:

(1) Events generated on the macro-level and affecting just the macro-level.

Examples are environmental events (like beginning to rain, strike of a lightning, collapse of a building, etc.). As the embedding of entities is defined on the macro-level, these type of events may also be used to model some kind of agent creation at a specific point in time and subsequent placement of new agents into the environment.

Events of this category do not directly influence the state space of entities, but only the environment $\mathbb{E}$ and, in case of agent creation, the entity set $\mathbb{ENT}$ and embedding *emb*.

(2) Events generated on the macro-level and directly affecting entities. Examples are events that represent perception (e. g., receiving a radio communication) as well as events resulting from conflicting actions of two agents as defined by model constraints (see Section 6.6.4).

(3) Events generated by an entity (in general by an agent) and affecting only the same entity.

This kind refers to the events used by the agents to control their own behavior (see Section 6.6.2).

Distinguishing the different event categories provides several benefits:

- Provide interface specifications
  Exogenous events associated with an agent (category (2) in Figure 6.5) serve as an interface specification and define precisely which event types an agent can process.

- Enable encapsulation and component-based development
  Defining interfaces is a necessary prerequisite to enable encapsulation (i. e., inner structure and behavior of an agent is irrelevant to

the overall model) and offers the possibility for component-based development. In this context, component refers to agents and objects
which may be modeled and implemented once and reused within
several simulation models, provided that the respective models
support the required event categories.

- Minimize potential conflicts
  Distinguishing the event categories helps to minimize potential
  conflicts. Events of different categories (e. g., endogenous events
  within the environment and within an agent) are decoupled and do
  not influence each other. Therefore, corresponding state transitions
  may be computed independently (and possibly in parallel) by a simulation engine without the need for synchronization. Furthermore,
  limiting the scope of events (e. g., to a single agent type) increases
  encapsulation and improves reusability. This aspect is especially
  important if development is done in a collaborative fashion and a
  global overview and management of event types is hardly achievable.

The set of all possible types of events which can possibly occur is
denoted by $\mathbb{EV}$. In other words, $\mathbb{EV}$ does not denote the actual events
themselves but all different types of events which are suitable and
required for a problem-specific model.

6.6 Micro-level modeling

This section describe the micro-level modeling of an agent-based
model which includes especially structure and behavior of single
agents. Generally speaking, any agent-based model consists of an
environment and multiple entities interacting in it. The term *entity*
refers to 'any object or component in the system which requires explicit
representation in the model' [16, p. 68]. An entity can either be an
agent or an object [137].

Definition 15 (Entity set) The set $\mathbb{ENT}$ denotes all entities which
are part of an agent-based model. $\mathbb{A}$ denotes the set of agents and $\mathbb{O}$
the set of objects with $\mathbb{ENT} = \mathbb{A} \cup \mathbb{O}$ and $\mathbb{A} \cap \mathbb{O} = \emptyset$.   □

As it is common agreement that an agent consists of a body and a behavior (cp. [114, 69]), this distinction is adopted for the GRAMS reference model:

Definition 16 (Agent) An *agent* $A \in \mathbb{A}$ is defined as tuple $A = (\mathbb{ATT}, \mathbb{SEN}, \mathbb{EFF})$ with $\mathbb{ATT}$ representing a set of attributes, $\mathbb{SEN}$ denoting the agents sensors and $\mathbb{EFF}$ being the set of effectors of this agent. □

As objects can be seen as agents without behavior, the definition of an object looks like a subset of the agent definition:

Definition 17 (Object) An *object* $O \in \mathbb{O}$ is defined by a set of attributes: $O = (\mathbb{ATT})$. □

Due to this similarity, objects are not explicitly treated in the following sections.

6.6.1 Attributes of agents and objects

Agents and objects are characterized by various properties (e. g., size, speed, temperature, mental attitudes, current beliefs). These properties are defined as set of attributes $\mathbb{ATT} = (b_1, \ldots, b_n)$ (cp. [16, p. 9]) where each attribute b_i may have values of a different domain B_i. The attributes are characterized as follows:

- Each attribute may be either static (e. g., size) or dynamic (e. g., speed). This distinction is dependent on the model purpose, e. g., size of an agent may be static or dynamic (depending on whether growth is modeled or not).

- Each attribute may be perceivable by other agents or not. In general this will depend on the attribute type and the sensoric capabilities of the other agents. For example, some agents may perceive temperatures while another kind of agent is incapable of perceiving temperatures.

As visibility of attributes depends on multiple factors, the GRAMS reference model does not distinguish further between *internal* and *external* attributes of an agent.

The domain of an attribute may be arbitrarily complex: an attribute may be described by a simple numerical value (e. g., length and width in meters), but it may also be described by complex data types (e. g., for representing knowledge of an agent). Of course, such complex data types may reference specific ontologies or standardized data models. In this context it is important to note that all knowledge stored internally by an agent (no matter how complex) is represented as attributes.

6.6.2 Sensors and effectors

On an informal basis the behavior of a single agent is determined by the following aspects:

- Each agent has a number of *sensors* $\mathbb{SEN}$ and *effectors* $\mathbb{EFF}$.

- All actions of an agent are represented by sensors and effectors.

- Each sensor or effector action may consume time.

- Sensors and effectors may trigger further sensor and effector actions.

- Multiple sensors and effectors may be active *simultaneously*.

This informal description of an agent does not include event handling. The occurrence of an event can influence an agent and usually triggers some kind of action within the agent. In the following, sensors and effectors are discussed in detail.

Definition 18 (Sensor) A *sensor* provides perception capabilities to an agent. A sensor

- may be triggered by exogenous and endogenous events

- and can trigger new endogenous events. □

Definition 19 (Effector) An *effector* provides capabilities to an agent for actively causing state changes. In contrast to sensors, an effector

- may only be triggered by endogenous events

- and can trigger endogenous as well as exogenous events. □

The sensors are primarily used by an agent for perceiving its environment. Each sensor may activate effectors of an agent or further sensors. Effectors may either alter the environment (e. g., picking up some object), affect an agents embedding within the environment (e. g., movement of an agent) or change an agents attributes (e. g., due to a *mental* action like reasoning).

Definition 20 (Action) An *action* refers to a sensor or effector which was triggered by an event and is currently active. □

In close analogy to the distinction made for event categories (see Section 6.5), sensors and effectors may also be distinguished as *exogenous* or *endogenous*:

- *Exogenous sensors* perceive information from the environment surrounding an agent. Obvious examples are optical sensors of any kind or an antenna to receive radio transmissions.

- *Endogenous sensors* may perceive information only from within an agent. Sensors of this type might be used to model situations where agents need sensors to monitor their own state (e. g., engine temperature). The decision whether an agent needs a sensor to monitor the state of its own properties (represented by the agents' attributes) depends on the model purpose and is completely up to the model developer.

- *Exogenous effectors* affect the environment surrounding an agent. An exogenous effector may directly alter the environment respectively an agents embedding within the environment (e. g., by a movement) or lead to the creation of appropriate events (e. g., if an agent sends a radio transmission, the simulation engine has to generate transmission events for the receiving agents).

- *Endogenous effectors* of an agent do not affect the surrounding environment but only an agent itself. These effectors are used to represent an agents' internal reasoner and affect an agents' internal attributes (e. g., due to a reasoning or planning process).

The actual behavior of an agent is therefore described by *sensor-effector-chains* which couple sensor and effector actions depending on the events received by an agent.

Definition 21 (Sensor-effector-chain) A *sensor-effector-chain* is a combination of sensors and effectors of an agent for the purpose of specifying its behavior.   □

The combination of sensors and effectors in a sensor-effector-chain is defined implicitly. Each sensor and effector may trigger endogenous events which in turn trigger another sensor or effector of an agent. Thus, a sensor-effector-chain is determined by the events triggered by the sensors and effectors of an agent.

As an example, Figure 6.6 illustrates event processing. From time t_0 to t_1 agent 2 activates one of his effectors (in this case, the send-effector) to send a radio transmission. At the end of the effector action, propagation of the radio signal begins. The communication range of agent 2 is indicated by the dashed circle; accordingly only agent 1 is within communication range. At time t_2 the radio signal has reached agent 1 and a receive-event is generated which agent 1 perceives with one of its sensors.

Example: Firespread Figure 6.7 illustrates the sensor-effector-chains of fireman-agent and firebug-agent. A fireman-agent possesses the following sensors and effectors:

- Perceive: Perception of the environment, duration: 1 time step

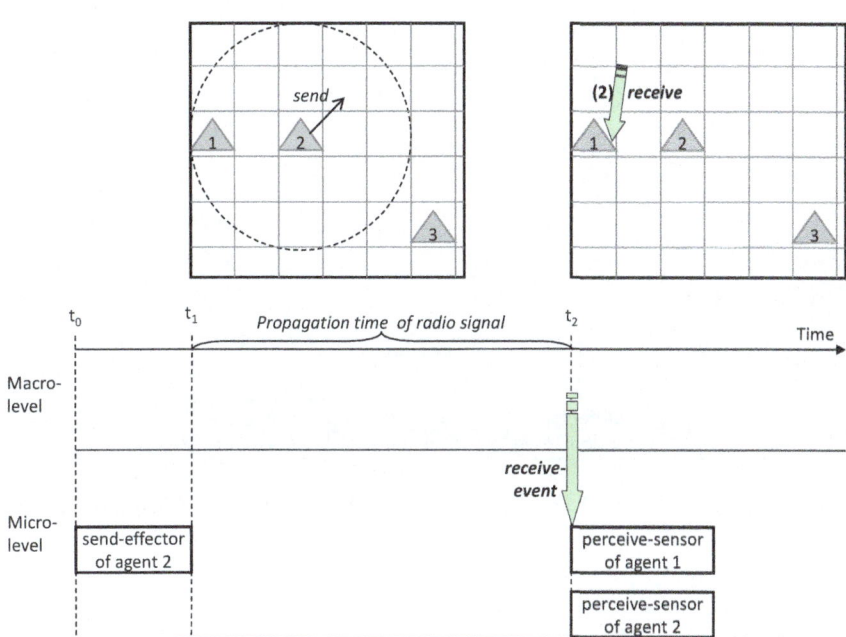

Figure 6.6: Example for effector action and event generation: Agent 2
sends a radio transmission at time t_1. Agent 1 is within communication range (indicated by dashed circle) and receives
the transmission at time t_2.

- Plan: Choose next action depending on current perception,
  duration: 1 time step

- Move: Move to a neighboring cell (in direction of closest fire),
  duration: 1 time step

- Water: Use water to extinguish fire on current cell, duration: 4
  time steps

The Plan-effector represents the internal reasoning process of the
agent. Taking into account the last perception, the fireman-agent

Fireman-agent:

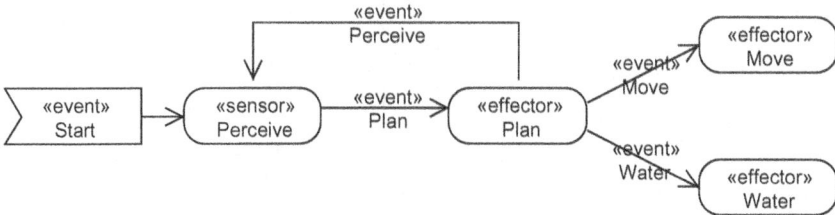

Firebug-agent:

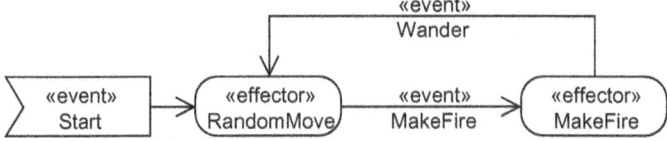

Figure 6.7: Firespread-example: Sensor-effector-chains of fireman-agent and firebug-agent.

decides whether to water a fire on the current cell, to move in direction of the closest fire, or to stay at the current position. In any case, the *main loop* of perceiving and planning is executed all the time.

The firebug-agent possesses the following effectors:

- RandomMove: Move randomly to a neighboring cell, duration: 1 time step

- MakeFire: Ignite current cell with probability 0.1, duration: 1 time step

The firebug-agent acts in a simple loop of randomly moving to a neighboring cell and trying to ignite the current cell. Only cells of type *forest* may be ignited.   ◁

6.6.3 State of an agent

The state $S_t(A)$ of an agent A at time t describes the totality of current attribute values as well as the current status of all sensors and effectors. Each attribute may have values from a different domain whereas sensors and effectors are either *active* or *inactive*. Therefore, the state of an agent A is defined as:

$$S_t(A) : \text{ATT} \times \text{SEN} \times \text{EFF} \to \quad (6.7)$$
$$(B_1 \times \cdots \times B_n) \times$$
$$\{inactive, active\}^{|\text{SEN}|} \times$$
$$\{inactive, active\}^{|\text{EFF}|}$$

6.6.4 Constraints

Constraints determine conditions under which successful execution of a sensor or effector action of an agent is possible and therefore represent general laws of the model world. The set of all constraints is denoted by $\mathbb{C}$. As they limit the agents behavior and the interaction of agents with the environment, constraints are concerned with the micro-level and the macro-level. Constraints are an essential part of an agent-based model and can be modeled in various ways (propositional logic, first-order logic, ...). It is assumed that all constraints are specified in an appropriate form and that they can be evaluated in the ways required by a simulation engine.

Formally, given an agent-based model M and a currently active sensor or effector x of an agent, a constraint $c \in \mathbb{C}$ is defined as follows:

$$c : S_t(M) \times x \to \{\text{true}, \text{false}\} \quad (6.8)$$

For each sensor or effector action x at any point in time t (i.e., for any state of the model M) the constraint c is currently fulfilled or not.

Two disjoint situations and intended purposes of constraints are distinguished:

1. Constraints as limiting (environmental) conditions
   Constraints are used to limit the possibility of an action to be
   executed successfully. Constraints of this type will most probably
   involve more than one action and define under which conditions
   two (or more) actions of different agents are influencing each other.
   Used with this intention, constraints are clearly an essential part
   of a model.

2. Constraints as assertions
   Constraints can also be used to assert specific properties. In
   this case, constraints might define which preconditions have to be
   fulfilled for execution of specific actions or, more generally, which
   conditions have to be fulfilled during the entire execution time of
   any action.

Depending on the specific constraint, the effect or consequence of an
unfulfilled (or violated) constraint may differ. Considering constraints
as limiting conditions, a violated constraint results in the creation of
a specific event. This event in turn may directly alter the involved
agents (e. g., limited mobility after a collision) and eventually the
corresponding location within the environment. In case of constraints
as assertions, which will most likely be used during development
or verification of a model, the possible response to an unfulfilled
constraint ranges from simply creating an entry in an error log to
aborting the current simulation (*fail-fast* behavior [119]).

The basic assumption is that no constraints are defined at all.
Therefore, all sensor and effector actions of an agent are always
executed successfully and no two actions interfere with each other.
Nevertheless, constraints are an integral part of an agent-based model
and may help a lot to increase overall quality of the model. This is
mainly due to two reasons:

- First, constraints are an appropriate and elegant way to make
  implicit assumptions explicit. Besides documenting assertions as
  well as pre- and post-conditions for specific actions, constraints
  allow to explicitly express these assumptions. Furthermore, this can

be done in a way that a simulation engine is capable of checking these assertions during a simulation execution.

- Secondly, constraints help to prevent erroneous agent behavior or at least to detect erroneous behavior at an early stage during model development. Especially if development is done collaboratively by different parties preventing erroneous behavior is important. By explicitly modeling constraints a simulation engine is capable of enforcing the constraints during a simulation execution. Thereby, flaws in the behavior or subtle errors in the implementation are detected fast and without manual support.

Besides preventing and detecting erroneous behavior constraints are also an appropriate way to increase and ensure a certain level of fairness between agents (as cheating is prevented).

Clearly, using constraints for the second reason is essentially done for verification and validation purposes. Therefore, constraints introduced for such purposes of verification and validation are not strictly part of a model itself, but part of the associated test suite of a model.

Example: Firespread Two constraints are defined:

- Limiting-Condition-Constraint: No more than one fireman-agent may water the same cell at the same time. If this is the case, the water supply is failing and all water-actions of the agents on this cell are aborted instantaneously.

- Assertion-Constraint: The firebug-agent may only ignite the cell it is currently occupying. If the firebug tries to ignite any other cell, the simulation will be aborted with an appropriate error message.

◁

6.6.5 Behavior of an agent

Recalling the given definitions, an agent is comprised of sensors and effectors which may be active in parallel. The behavior of an agent A is defined as response to (exogenous and endogenous) events. An agent may receive an event due to two different circumstances: while endogenous events are tied to a specific agent, exogenous events may be perceived by a number of agents (depending on their sensors and embedding in the environment). Once an agent receives an event, the corresponding sensors and effectors are activated.

Definition 22 (Behavior of an agent) Given an agent A receiving at time $t_0 \in \mathbb{T}$ an event e of an event type defined in $\mathbb{EV}$. The behavior of A is defined as:

1. Let X_{act} be the subset of sensors and effectors of agent A which are activated by event e. Formally: $X_{act} = \bigcup_{x \in \text{SEN} \cup \text{EFF} | e \text{ activates } x} x$.

2. Each sensor and effector $x \in X_{act}$ is activated by event e at time t_0. Each active sensor and effector has to comply with the following specifications:

    a) Ensure compliance with given constraints
       The sensor or effector x is active in the interval $[t_0, t_1]$, i. e., action x starts at t_0 and ends at t_1. During the whole time it has to be ensured that all constraints defined within the model M are fulfilled:

    $$success = \bigwedge_{\forall t \in [t_0, t_1]: \forall c \in \mathbb{C}} c(M_t, x) \qquad (6.9)$$

       $success$ becomes false if any constraint is violated in the interval $[t_0, t_1]$.

    b) Two scenarios are possible for finishing the sensor or effector action x (cp. Figure 6.8):

       • $success = $ true: The sensor or effector x finishes successfully at t_1 and the model state as well as the agent state are altered accordingly.

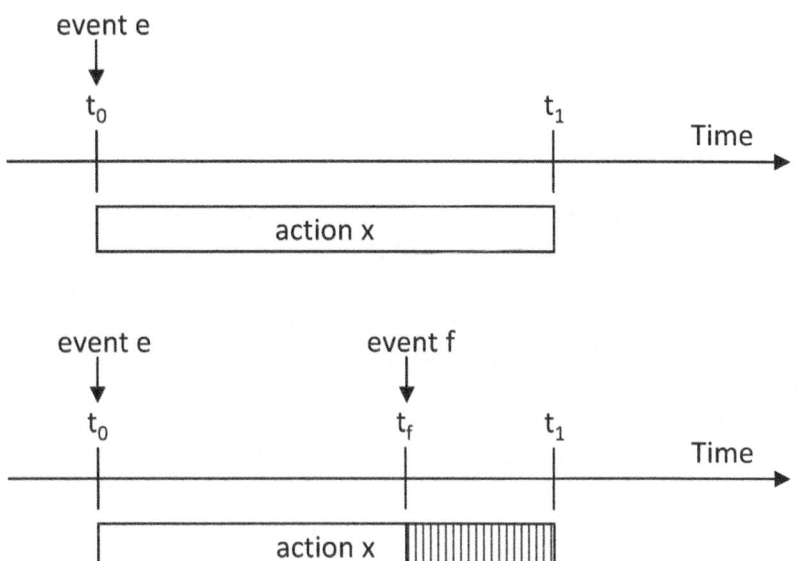

Figure 6.8: Successful (top) and unsuccessful (bottom) sensor or effector action x.

- *success* = false: Due to a constraint violation, action x does not finish successfully. In general, a constraint violation will trigger a corresponding *conflict-event* f. This event will be scheduled at t_f with t_f denoting the point in time where the first constraint violation occured. In this case, the sensor or effector action x is interrupted by an event f at time t_f ($t_0 \leq t_f < t_1$). The action x fails and the states of model and agent are altered depending on event f.

Constraints used for validation and verification purposes may behave different. They are not restrained to just triggering an event but may for example lead to an immediate abortion of the current simulation. This kind of special behavior is not considered here. □

By this definition, each sensor or effector action x either succeeds or fails. If an action starts in t_0 and if it finishes successfully, it terminates at $t_1 = t_0 + t^{\mathrm{succ}}(x)$ with $t^{\mathrm{succ}}(x)$ denoting the duration of the sensor or effector action x. If x fails, the action is aborted at $t_f = t_0 + t^{\mathrm{fail}}(x)$ with $t^{\mathrm{fail}}(x)$ denoting how long x has been executed before finally failing due to a constraint violation. It is important to remember that an action can only fail by means of influences from outside, i.e., by violation of some constraint (e.g., some conflict with an action of another agent).

In general, each sensor or effector action x (either successful or failed) implies state changes:

$$S_t(M) \times x \longrightarrow S_{t+t(x)}(M) \tag{6.10}$$

The actual nature of this state change, especially in case of failed actions is defined by the constraints of a model. A possible set of constraints could define that actions are executed as a whole or not at all. Another possibility would be to compute the result of a partial execution of an action x if x failed.

6.7 Simulation of an agent-based model

The GRAMS reference model requires that a simulation engine adheres to the given definitions and assures that all events are processed in accordance with the following definition. No further requirements are imposed on how to implement event handling.

Definition 23 (Processing an event) For an agent-based model M, an event e occurring at time $t \in \mathbb{T}$ is processed as follows:

- If e is of category *endogenous, on macro-level* (1), the environment is either directly altered or the appropriate update functions are triggered.

- If e is of category *exogenous, affecting agents* (2), the following procedure applies:

1. For each agent $A \in \mathbb{A}$ the set of all event types which activate a sensor or effector of agent A is denoted by $\mathbb{EV}^A_{activate}$. This set is the union of all event types which activate a sensor or effector of this agent: $\mathbb{EV}^A_{activate} = \bigcup_{e \in \mathbb{EV} | x \in \mathbb{SEN} \cup \mathbb{EFF} \wedge e \text{ activates } x} e$.

2. All agents $A \in \mathbb{A}$ with $e \in \mathbb{EV}^A_{activate}$ receive event e at time t and are executed according to Definition 22 (thereby taking into account the constraints defined within the model). □

- If e is of category *endogenous, within an agent* (3), the same procedure as for category (2) applies with the only difference that only the current agent receives the event.

This definition assures that each event e is relayed without delay to all agents able to respond to this event. All further processing is already defined by the behavior of a single agent.

Given the definition of an agent-based model, the *simulation* of such a model can now be defined:

Definition 24 (Multi-Agent Simulation) The simulation S of an agent-based model $M = (\mathbb{T}, \mathbb{E}, \mathbb{ENT}, emb, \mathbb{EV}, \mathbb{C})$ with respect to a specific time interval $[t_0, t_1] \in \mathbb{T}$ is defined as the processing of all events $\{e_1, \ldots, e_n\} \subseteq \mathbb{EV}$ occurring within this time interval. □

Therefore, if model M is in state M_0 at t_0 and M_1 at t_1, a simulation is the state transition $S : M_0 \times \{e_1, \ldots, e_n\} \rightarrow M_1$ of the underlying model.

The actual state of a model is the Cartesian product of all states of its entities. The events defined by the GRAMS reference model primarily trigger sensor and effector actions of the agents. These sensor and effector actions are then responsible for all state changes. In other words, although the events within the multi-agent simulation trigger some sensor or effector action, they are not the original source of progress.

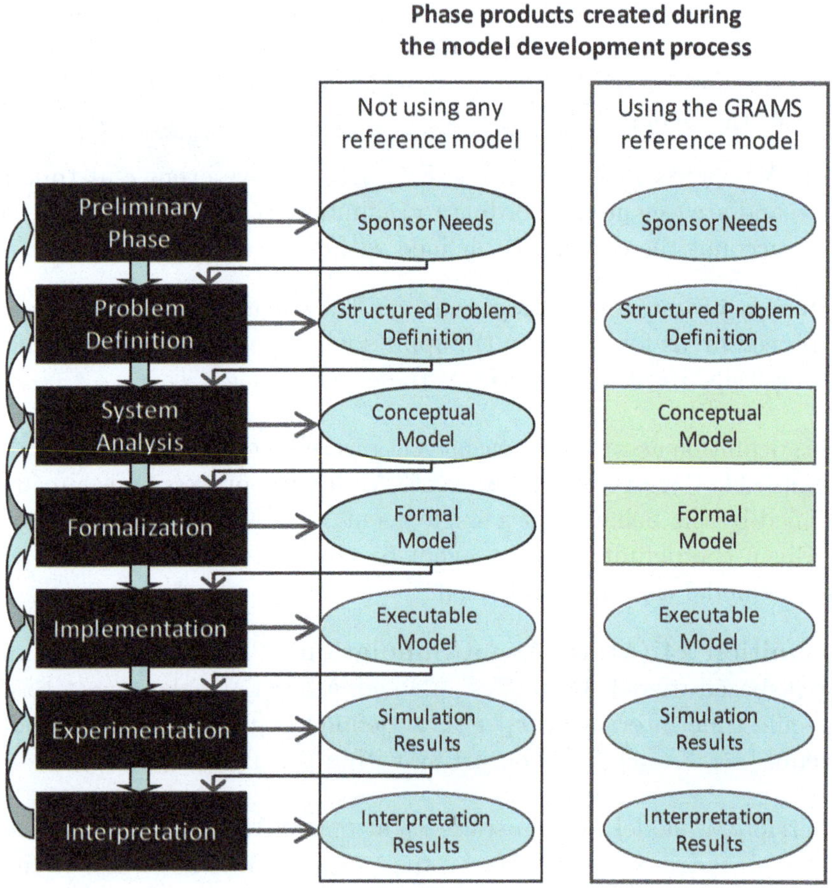

Figure 6.9: The GRAMS reference model supports the *System Analysis* and *Formalization* phases of a model development process.

6.8 Application areas of the GRAMS reference model

This section discusses the application areas for which the GRAMS reference model may be used. Primarily, the GRAMS reference model supports the development of conceptual models. Additionally it may guide the development of formal models as well and can therefore be applied in two phases of a model development process (see Figure 6.9):

- While developing a *conceptual model* the GRAMS reference model acts as a guideline for model developers. It helps to ensure that all important aspects are thought of and that they are documented in a uniform way. Thus, the GRAMS reference model helps to create a better common understanding between the involved model developers and may prevent misunderstandings. The common understanding of a model and its documentation enables and improves reuse of single model components and forms the basis for V&V-activities.

- Similarly, the GRAMS reference model provides a (semi-) formal description of an agent-based model and its simulation. Just as providing guidance for developing conceptual models, the GRAMS reference model provides guidance for developing *formal models*. The GRAMS reference model does not impose the use of a specific formalism, but leaves this decision open to the developers.

Ideally, the ideas laid out in the GRAMS reference model are strictly followed in an implementation. The transformation from a conceptual or formal model to an executable model could easily be done and benefits could be fully exploited (e. g., a strict separation of model and simulation engine allows to execute the same model on different simulation engines).

The GRAMS reference model is quite abstract on the conceptual level and is not constrained by any formalization- or implementation-specific issues. This may be illustrated by an example regarding the definition of simulation time. Whereas for a specific model, it may be completely sufficient to define simulation time on a conceptual level as continuous, this specification may be refined during the formalization phase to real numbers. Regarding the executable model, implementation-specific issues have to taken into account (e. g., time may be discretized and represented as an integer).

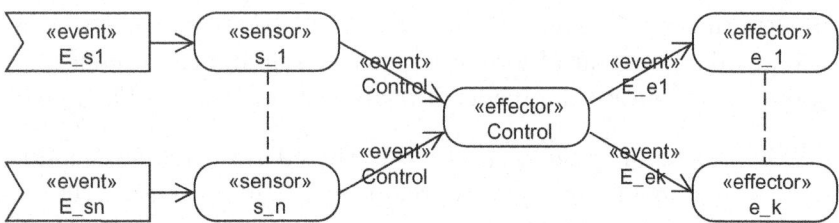

Figure 6.10: Mapping of a reactive agent architecture onto the GRAMS reference model.

6.9 Evaluation

In this section the applicability of the GRAMS reference model is evaluated. Firstly, it is demonstrated how basic agent architectures are modeled in terms of the GRAMS reference model. Secondly, the practical applicability of the GRAMS reference model is evaluated using three case studies. Finally, a brief summary of the evaluation results is given.

6.9.1 Mapping of basic agent architectures

The GRAMS reference model is intended as building block for more sophisticated abstractions. In order to demonstrate this property of the GRAMS reference model, three basic agent architectures (reactive, deliberative, and reflective agent architectures) which represent a broad range of agent architectures currently often used are mapped onto the GRAMS reference model. An overview over a broad variety of agent architectures may be found in [90].

Reactive agent architectures

Reactive agents are characterized by two aspects:

1. Reactive agents do not possess an internal model of the world.

2. The behavior is completely determined by the latest sensor input, i. e., they react directly to their current sensor inputs.

Given these characteristics, reactive agents can easily be modeled within the frame of the GRAMS reference model. The agent $A_{\text{reactive}} = (\text{ATT}, \text{SEN}, \text{EFF})$ is specified as follows (see Figure 6.10):

- ATT denotes the agents' properties (e. g., state of the agent).

- SEN $= \{s_1, \ldots, s_n\}$ denotes the agents' set of sensors.

- EFF $= \{Control, e_1, \ldots, e_k\}$ denotes the agents' set of effectors. The *Control*-effector is designated to choosing an appropriate effector e_i depending on the current sensor input. Each sensor action consists of processing the actual sensor input, followed by generating a *Control*-event in order to trigger the *Control*-effector. The *Control*-effector in turn decides which effector e_i has to be triggered (depending on the sensor input).

Defined this way, the mapping reflects very closely the *Sense-Reason-Act* cycle used in many agent architectures (cp. [30]).

Deliberative agent architectures

In contrast to reactive agent architectures, deliberative agents are characterized by an explicit internal world model and (sophisticated) reasoning and planning capabilities. Perhaps the most widely used deliberative agent architecture is the BDI-architecture. The main components of this architecture are *B*eliefs, *D*esires and *I*ntentions of an agent.

Beliefs represent an agents knowledge about the world which may be incomplete or imperfect. *Desires* represent the long-term goals of an agent. As such they are an integral part of the deliberative behavior and heavily influence an agents actions. Once an agent has commited itself to a goal, it has to select the next action. Usually, the agent is equipped with a plan library from which the plan is chosen which fits best to its current goal. The actually chosen plan which an agent executes is its *intention*. Simply said, desires represent long-term goals while intentions represent short-term goals which directly lead to a sequence of actions.

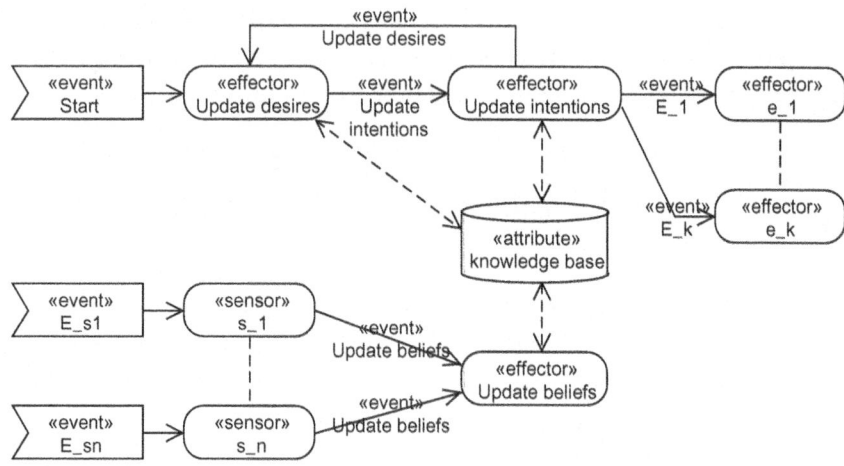

Figure 6.11: Mapping of a deliberative (BDI-inspired) agent architecture onto the GRAMS reference model.

The deliberation process of a BDI-agent usually consists of multiple steps [141, p. 58]: The belief revision function takes the current sensor input as well as beliefs and updates the agents' set of beliefs. The option generation function determines available options (desires), based on beliefs and desires. The set of current intentions is updated and finally an action is selected which is performed next.

Modeling deliberative agents within the frame of the GRAMS reference model is not unlike representing reactive agents as described previously. Following the *Sense-Reason-Act*-cycle, Figure 6.11 outlines the basic mapping of a deliberative agent architecture onto the GRAMS reference model.

The main difference to reactive agents is the explicit modeling of an agents internal knowledge. The *knowledge base* depicted in Figure 6.11 simply refers to a set of attributes b_i which are associated with this kind of agent. With respect to Section 6.6.1, the knowledge base is defined as follows:

$$knowledge\ base = (b_1, \ldots, b_n) \subseteq \text{ATT} \qquad (6.11)$$

As a single attribute b_i may be arbitrary complex, the plan library of a BDI-agent may also be represented within this knowledge base. For simplicity and clarity, the mapping illustrated in Figure 6.11 simplifies the deliberation process and shows only the two actions *Update desires* and *Update intentions*. It is of course possible to break these actions down into more specific actions which are then executed sequentially. This refinement may be applied to improve modularisation or reusability of single components.

Furthermore, each possible action of a BDI-agent is represented by a corresponding effector. As mentioned previously for reactive agents, the *Update intentions*-action has to generate specific events in order to trigger the desired effectors.

Reflective agent architectures

In addition to deliberative agents, reflective agents are capable of reflecting their choices and learning from the outcomes of previous actions. In other words, reflective agents are capable of adapting their behavior according to the results of previous actions and their perceptions of the effects of specific actions. Referring to Sloman, reflective agents are among the most sophisticated agent architectures [123].

Representing a reflective agent architecture within the GRAMS reference model may be achieved (at least) in the following way: Building upon the BDI-agent described previously, an agent must additionally be capable of altering its knowledge base (including its plan library) and to modify its sensor-effector-chains accordingly.

In the most simple case, the functionality to alter the plan library may be part of an already existing *reason*-action. Instead of only choosing the next action, an agent would also have to evaluate his former actions and thus reflect on previous choices. Once an agent has decided to change its behavior, the agent's sensor-effector-chains have to be altered accordingly. As these chains are not defined in a permanent way but represent the logical order of activating sensors and effectors by means of (endogenous) events, this modification just requires creating appropriate events.

6.9.2 Case studies

For evaluating the practical applicability of the GRAMS reference model, three applications were analyzed. The resulting simulation models were developed according to the GRAMS reference model. The complexity of the modeling task was increased continuously. The first case study considered a simple warehouse scenario and was used for basic evaluation purposes. The second case study considered a military scenario with increased interaction of agents and was developed jointly with Christian Gerstner [40, 41, 42]. A third application of the GRAMS reference model considered coordination of rescue units due to a massive traffic accident and involved a wide variety of different agent types and complex interaction patterns. This application was developed jointly with Daniel Weyel [142].

As a first step within the evaluation of the GRAMS reference model, a small but typical case study was analyzed using the GRAMS reference model. This case study considers a simplified warehouse scenario (2-dimensional environment) including three different types of agents (worker, forklift, warehouse manager) with limited interaction. A detailed description of the simulation model is given in appendix A.1.

The GRAMS reference model provided a valuable guideline throughout the development process. Regarding this case study, the GRAMS reference model could be applied very well and did not impose any unnecessary or limiting constraints. Regarding the experiences gained from the first case study, two issues are worth mentioning:

- First, as defined by the GRAMS reference model, all sensor and effector actions are triggered by corresponding events. Especially in case of sensor-effector sequences which are repeatedly executed (e. g., a typical main loop) or do not depend on exogenous events, introducing (possibly a multitude of) events to control behavior of an agent can be irritating at first. Once one gets used to this kind of modeling, the simple but strict principle – each sensor and effector action is triggered by an event – seems quite natural and rewards model developers with a strict interface defining precisely input and output of an agent.

- Second, quite similar to the first issue, explicitly modeling constraints under which an effector action is successful or fails is uncommon at first. As usual, model developers tend to neglect the value of introducing explicit constraints on the grounds that they are unnecessary if a model is built correctly. But this reasoning is deceptive as most errors and flaws are introduced unintentionally. Explicitly modeling constraints has proven to be very useful.

Multiple interactions between agents of different types presented a new challenge, when developing the second case study which considers a specific military scenario (see appendix A.2 for more details). In this case, the most difficult part of model development was to ensure correct coordination between agents. Modeling various information exchange relations and subsequent actions to be carried out by the agents was a challenging task. Even though only three different types of agents are considered, it was sometimes difficult to keep track of the intricate interplay of mutiple agents.

Like in the first case study, the GRAMS reference model served very well as a guideline throughout the development process. The strict seperation of events and actions defined by the GRAMS reference model turned out to be helpful also. This separation allowed the construction of complex agent behaviors where each event could trigger different actions at the same time.

While being beneficial, this caused trouble at the same time. In fact, it turned out that effects of an event are intricate to analyze and debug. This is not necessarily a drawback of the GRAMS reference model, but has at least two reasons: First, the example implementation and the tool chain available did not support all aspects of the GRAMS reference model very well and provided only few debugging features. Second, and perhaps more notably, modeling sophisticated interaction patterns may exhibit a certain immanent complexity.

The third application deals with representing coordination efforts between multiple rescue units due to a massive traffic accident. After an accident is reported a coordinating office has to order available units (like police, emergency doctor, fire fighters and towing service) to the scene of the accident. Once arrived, the first unit at the scene takes over command and is responsible for coordinating all units currently at the scene of the accident. In order to analyze the impact of inaccurate information (e. g., an emergency call with imprecise information about number of cars and persons involved in the accident), a simulation model was developed [142]. During this model development effort the GRAMS reference model was used and thus information about the practical applicability of the GRAMS reference model was gained.

The GRAMS reference model was a very valuable development guideline ensuring that all critical issues are thought of. Furthermore, the GRAMS reference model also served as a guideline in which order certain modeling tasks should be done. Especially for less experienced model developers (as was the case in this model development effort), this guidance is very helpful. Even the largely increased number of agent types and interactions which implies an increased number of event types and information exchange relations between agents could be handled in an efficient way.

In summary, the GRAMS reference model served well as a guideline for developing agent-based models of complex systems. Although most (if not all) considerations made within the process of developing agent-based models would have to be done anyway regardless if the GRAMS reference model is used or not, there are at least two benefits in using the GRAMS reference model. First of all, following the GRAMS reference model ensures that all important points are considered. At least, the possibility of forgetting important issues is reduced. Second, having a suitable reference model at hand eases transition from individual, incomparable model development processes (and model documentation) towards a more standardized procedure. This may result in more comparable results and documentation.

7 Summary

Though agent-based modeling and simulation receives a lot of attention, understanding and interpretation varies and many issues are still unresolved. Most notably, agent-based modeling is neither a revolutionary new modeling paradigm nor a silver bullet for all modeling tasks. The reasons why agent-based modeling receives so much attention are manifold:

1. Agent-based models are very well suited to represent complex systems with many individually acting entities (like social systems). They allow a structurally very similar representation of a system under investigation by a model, thus easing understanding as well as communication between domain experts and model developers.

2. Agent-based models stress micro-level modeling and encapsulation of agent structure and behavior. Interaction and communication between agents is often well-understood on a microscopic and individual level which simplifies model development. Encapsulation improves reusability and thus also improves model development processes.

3. Agent-based models are easily scalable in number of agents and in level of detail regarding agent behavior.

Finally, agent-based modeling and simulation is intimately connected with the availability of computing power necessary for simulating large-scale models.

Despite high attention and lots of work in the area of agent-based modeling and simulation, a common understanding of basic terms is often not given. A generally accepted agreement on what constitutes an agent-based model is missing, as well as precise definitions of the simulation of an agent-based model. This leads to the unsatisfactory situation that the result of a simulation is often less dependend on the model itself than on the currently used simulation engine.

In order to overcome these problems, the *General Reference Model for Agent-based Modeling and Simulation* (GRAMS) is proposed. The GRAMS reference model provides a domain-independent framework for agent-based modeling and simulation.

The GRAMS reference model focuses primarily on the development of conceptual models and may also guide development of formal models. It provides precise definitions of key concepts of agent-based models and specifies interrelations and dependencies of model components, and finally defines the simulation of an agent-based model. In this respect, the GRAMS reference model consolidates existing definitions and puts them into an integrated framework. As a conceptual reference model the GRAMS reference model is defined in a way that imposes as few as possible constraints on the development of actual problem-specific models.

Besides simplifying actual development processes by using the GRAMS reference model as a template, understandability, traceability, verification and validation, and reuse of models may be improved due to increased comparability of models. The GRAMS reference model defines basic concepts of agent-based modeling and simulation and thus provides a low-level modeling approach. More sophisticated concepts like specific agent architectures and protocols for multi-agent interactions may be based on the GRAMS reference model.

For evaluation purposes, a representation of three basic agent architectures within the GRAMS reference model is outlined (reactive agents, deliberative agents and reflective agents). Furthermore, three case studies have been analyzed to evaluate the practical applicability of the GRAMS reference model. Regarding these case studies, the GRAMS reference model can be applied effectively for conceptual model development and does not impose any unnecessary or limiting constraints. On the contrary, the evaluation results indicate that the GRAMS reference model provides a valuable guideline throughout a model development process.

Regarding potential speedup of a simulation execution by exploiting model-inherent parallelism, the possibility to execute a model on different simulation engines with identical results is a prerequisite. Part III of this thesis defines various model partitioning strategies and proposes a hierarchical model of parallel execution. Practical applicability is demonstrated by an example implementation and selected empirical measurements.

Part III

Effective model execution

8 Model partitioning and multi-level parallelization

Effective execution of an agent-based model refers to utilization of hardware resources for improvement of performance or reliability and involves two aspects:

1. Model partitioning
   At first, an agent-based model has to be decomposed into partitions with minimum interaction.

2. Parallel execution
   Once a model is decomposed into partitions, a simulation engine for executing the model may be parallelized. Ideally, the number of parallel computing threads equals the number of model partitions.

The combination of model partitioning and parallelized execution is illustrated in Figure 8.1. Details on both aspects are presented in the following sections.

8.1 Model partitioning strategies

The key to achieving performance improvements is to partition a model in such a way that interactions between partitions are minimized and therefore concurrent execution of model partitions by independent computing threads is possible.

8.1.1 Terms and definitions

The distinction between macro-level modeling and micro-level modeling is adopted for characterizing different model partitioning strategies:

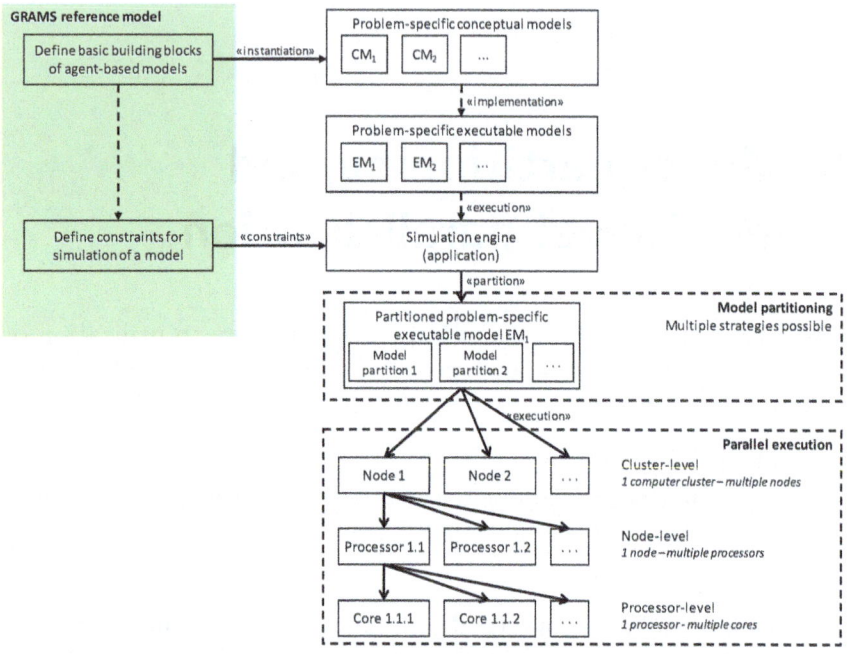

Figure 8.1: Model partitioning and multi-level parallelization.

- Partitioning on macro-level
  As the environment is a central element of agent-based models, the environment has to be considered carefully for each partitioning strategy. This is especially true, if multiple computing nodes can be utilized. Two basic alternatives are *partitioning* the environment or *replicating* the environment. Partitioning the environment requires that the environment is split up and distributed onto the available computing nodes. Replicating the environment requires that the environment is replicated on all computing nodes and only agents or actions are distributed onto the available nodes.

- Partitioning on micro-level
  Partitioning on micro-level mainly concerns the decomposition of the set of agents. Two different approaches can easily be devised:

- The obvious choice is to partition on a *per-agent*-basis. This way, all issues related to the simulation of one agent are concentrated within one partition and subsequently within one thread. This thread in turn may be responsible for multiple agents, of course.

- A second possibility is to partition on a *per-action*-basis. This approach does not consider agents as a whole, but treats sensor and effector actions of all agents individually. Actions which do not interfere with each other may be executed concurrently. The main problem of this approach is that access to shared memory of a single agent may be distributed across multiple partitions (and subsequently across multiple threads).

Many more partitioning strategies may be thought of, yet these are the basic strategies. The crucial aspect of all partitioning strategies is the identification of actions or agents which are independent of each other and may therefore be executed concurrently.

Despite the partitioning strategy (*How?*) the partition computation strategy (*When?*) or update rate of a partitioning has to be considered:

- A *static* partitioning is computed once at the beginning of a simulation and only updated when necessary (e. g., new agents joining a simulation). The main benefit of this computation strategy is its simplicity, which on the other side may lead to suboptimal parallelization. This is due to at least two reasons: An ideal partitioning may not be known in advance (i. e., without running a simulation), and an ideal partitioning may change over time.

- A *dynamic* partitioning is updated regularly (either in fixed time intervals or due a specific condition). This computation strategy may take into account much more information than a static computation strategy. Based on statistic information gathered during a simulation, an ideal partitioning may be determined. Also, changes in a model during simulation (like agents joining and leaving a model) may be taken into account. A drawback of this strategy is the considerably more complex implementation. Furthermore, updating a partitioning costs time and has to be evaluated against the benefits gained by an improved partitioning.

In summary, static and dynamic partition computation strategies represent different update rates ranging from once during a simulation (static) to multiple updates during a simulation (dynamic). Additionally, dynamic partition computation strategies may exploit statistical knowledge gained during a simulation.

The quality of a specific partitioning depends on many factors. Obviously, a partitioning is considered better if the runtime for a simulation is reduced as far as possible. Unfortunately, it is not easy to tell in advance which strategy is best. Strategies may be devised to distribute agents or actions uniformly across partitions (assuming this results in maximized parallelism and therefore maximum speedup) or to partition a model in a way that communication between nodes is minimized (assuming network connections between nodes are limiting elements). Although all these assumptions and considerations may be correct, it is impossible to estimate in advance which strategy produces the best results. As dynamics of a model change during execution of a simulation, it is very likely that at different points in time different partitions are most suited. Similar questions are also addressed by research in the areas of load balancing [29, 118, 32] and online algorithms [7].

In the following, different partitioning strategies covering a wide range of issues discussed in this section are specified. The available computing nodes are denoted by $N_1 \ldots N_m$. Each node i may execute n_i threads concurrently, and subsequently the available threads for each node N_i are denoted by $T_1^i \ldots T_{n_i}^i$. If only one node is considered the superscript i indicating the node is dropped, hence the available threads are denoted by $T = \{T_1 \ldots T_n\}$.

8.1.2 Conflict detection as bottleneck

The GRAMS reference model defines simulation as a sequence of state transitions. The computation of a state transition takes only into account the current model state and an event which has to be executed (see Chapter 6.7). Independently of how much simulation time has already elapsed a simulation engine is always faced with an identical task of computing follow-up states. The computation of a state transition always takes the same amount of wallclock time and therefore runtime grows almost linearly with elapsed simulation time. Although the computation of state changes associated with any successfully executed action accounts for a great deal of the overall runtime, the potentially more crucial aspect is the evaluation of constraints defined within an agent-based model (see Chapter 6.6.4).

As constraint evaluation takes up to $O(n_A^2)$ runtime (with n_A referring to the number of agents) it has a very dominant influence on overall runtime (cp. [48]). Assuming that all n_A agents have at least one effector and that all effectors take one time step to execute, n_A effector actions are executed simultaneously. Assuming further that only one constraint is defined which determines whether an effector action may be executed or not (depending on the other effector actions), each action a needs to be checked against $n_A - 1$ other actions which results in $n_A \times (n_A - 1)$ constraint evaluations. Even assuming symmetry reduces this number only to $\frac{1}{2}(n_A^2 - n_A)$ and therefore runtime of constraint evaluation is expected to be quadratic in the number of agents n_A.

In order to achieve reasonable speedups quadratic growth in runtime needs to be avoided [125]. Given the nature of the constraints and the inherent possibility of actions to interfere with each other, evaluating constraints of n agents, respectively actions, results in quadratic runtime. In this case, the best possible solution is to largely reduce the number n of agents or actions which may interfere with each other. This way quadratic runtime is still required, but only for small numbers n of actions. Reducing the numbers of evaluations whether two or more actions are interfering can mainly be achieved by the following two means:

- Spatial decomposition
  By separating non-interfering agents and actions spatially, only agents and actions within the same spatial region need to be checked for interference.

- Action-dependent decomposition
  This approach exploits the fact that only specific actions may interfere (e. g., two *walk*-actions may interfere, but not a *walk*-action and a *communicate*-action). At this point, the hypothesis is that most actions do not interfere with each other. Of course, worst-case complexity is still $O(n^2)$, yet it is expected that in average n is quite low.

Computing a partitioning in such a way that interaction between partitions is minimized (i. e., no interference of actions due to constraints), is equivalent to the graph partitioning problem which is known to be NP-hard [38, p. 209]. A good survey of heuristic algorithms for solving the graph partitioning problem is given in [65].

Partitioning strategies based on spatial decomposition and action-dependent decomposition are described more detailed in the following subsections.

8.1.3 Partitioning strategy: node-level, per agent, static

This partitioning strategy aims at node-level parallelization and considers partitioning on a *per-agent*-basis with a static computation of the partitioning. Due to static partitioning no information regarding dynamic behavior (i. e., which agents interact respectively interfere with each other) is taken into account. Algorithm 1 illustrates the basic principle of this partitioning strategy. All agents are distributed uniformly to the available threads T. The partitioning is basically a mapping of each agent to the thread by which its actions are computed. As no specific information is taken into account this partitioning strategy is also characterized as *uninformed*.

Algorithm 1 Partitioning strategy *node-level, per agent, static.*

Require: Set of agents $\mathbb{A} = \{A_1, \ldots, A_m\}$
Require: Set of available threads $T = \{T_0, \ldots, T_{n-1}\}$
    Define partition as mapping from agents to threads: *partition* : $\mathbb{A} \to T$
    threadIndex $= 0$
    for all agents $A \in \mathbb{A}$ **do**
        partition$(A) := T_{\text{threadIndex}}$
        threadIndex $= (\text{threadIndex} + 1) \mod n$
    end for
    return *partition*

8.1.4 Partitioning strategy: node-level, per agent, dynamic

In contrast to the static partitioning strategy described above, a dynamic partitioning strategy takes into account context information. This may result in a better partitioning of a model and thus in reduced runtime. The key question to be answered for such an *informed* partitioning strategy is which measure should be used for evaluating the *quality* of a partition. As indicated earlier the quality of a partitioning is finally determined by the achieved overall speedup of a simulation. Indirectly, the quality of a partition may be measured very differently, e.g., distributing agents as uniformly as possible, distributing agents based on a proximity measure, or even taking into account past or future interaction between agents. Keeping in mind that quadratic runtime (imposed by constraint evaluation) needs to be dealt with, reducing the number of possibly interfering actions is of high importance.

In dynamic partitioning strategies a partition is computed initially and updated during a simulation. The decision when to update a partition depends on the chosen partitioning strategy as well as on the dynamics of the current simulation. Therefore, each dynamic partitioning strategy has to define two functions:

1. `informed(`$\mathbb{A}, T, s, p$`)`
   Creates an initial partitioning or updates an existing partitioning. The function takes the set of agents $\mathbb{A}$, the set of available threads T, the partitioning strategy s, and an eventually existing partitioning p as input. It returns a new partitioning.

2. `updateNecessary(`p`)`
   Evaluates whether the current partitioning p has to be updated or not.

Additional information is required to evaluate whether an update of a partitioning is necessary or not, and to actually compute an updated partitioning. Collection and computation of this (statistical) information are not included in the functions mentioned above, but will be described in context of specific partitioning strategies.

Besides these two functions, the constraint evaluation has to be adapted to make use of the additional information. Each partitioning strategy will therefore require a specific adapted function for evaluating constraints.

Spatial decomposition

Spatial decomposition aims at reducing the number of evaluations whether two or more actions are interfering by spatial separation. The improvement gained by this separation is that only actions within the same spatial region need to be checked for interference.

Known approaches include the *Spheres of Influence* proposed by Logan and Theodoropolous [78, 127] and the notion of *Event Horizons* by Scheutz and Schermerhorn [114]. Steinman also follows this approach and proposes a so-called 'grid-based publish and subscribe data distribution system' [125]. This approach is similar to using well-known quad-trees or oct-trees for spatial representation of a model. One challenge is to determine the size of the grid which is equivalent to determining number and layout of spatial regions respectively partitions [125].

A tacit assumption often made when using spatial decomposition is that it is possible to split a model (environment and agents) into the required number of partitions. The maximum number of partitions is usually determined by the number of threads that may be executed in parallel. To exploit maximal parallelism, a model has to be split up into the same number of disjoint partitions. In this context, *disjoint* refers to partitions of a model which do not influence each other (i. e., agents of the respective partitions do not interfere with each other). Although spatial decomposition is often used with good results [125, 97, 78, 114], it may be impossible or inefficient to compute the necessary number of disjoint partitions for a wide variety of agent-based models.

At least two different types of spatial decomposition are conceivable:

1. *Informed* spatial decomposition
   As mentioned above, the set of agents is split into disjoint sets which can not influence each other as they are too far apart and thus belong to different spatial regions.

2. *Uninformed* spatial decomposition
   A second approach is to specify spatial regions in advance without taking into account context information. Each region is assigned to a separate computing thread which takes care of all agents within this region. Obviously, this approach will most probably not produce an optimal decomposition of the set of agents. However, this approach is easy to implement and introduces only minimal overhead for computing an initial partitioning and updating the mapping of agents to specific spatial regions.

Action-dependent decomposition

An alternative to partitioning a model along spatial boundaries is to partition the currently executed actions according to their type. This partitioning strategy aims at executing those actions simultaneously by different threads which are not able to interfere with each other due to their nature. In general, many types of actions are very different in nature and simply can not interfere with each other. This may, for example, be the case for actions which affect the environment and actions which represent internal reasoning processes of an agent.

Combined decomposition

Obviously, the two basic approaches presented may be combined. Using spatial decomposition and action-dependent decomposition in a combined fashion may circumvent the problem of splitting a model into disjoint sets. In a first step, spatial decomposition may be used to split a model into few (large) partitions. Secondly, the resulting partitions may be further split up using action-dependent decomposition.

The main benefit of combined decomposition is that it is easy and allows fast computation. On the negative side, combined decomposition may not always exploit the maximal possible parallelism. The total number of threads used by this approach is $g \times a_g$ (with g the number of spatial regions and a_g the number of partitions resulting from action-dependent decomposition within region g). If it is not possible to compute the required number of action-independent partitions (e. g., due to a huge number of interfering types of actions), some of the available threads may remain idle.

Self-optimizing decomposition

A further approach for partitioning a model is to employ methods and techniques of self-optimization. The main problem of all partitioning strategies is that the quality of a partitioning can only be evaluated afterwards. In general, this is done by measuring the runtime and evaluating whether the current partitioning strategy led to significant speedup. All attempts to evaluate the partitioning in advance are of secondary value. This is because the measurement of direct indicators (like e. g., equality of distribution of agents to partitions, minimization of agent interaction, minimization of network traffic, etc.) which may be computed for a partitioning do not predict the actual reduction of runtime.

Choosing an appropriate indicator to deduce runtime improvements is usually only possible if the currently executed model and its behavior are well-known. Based on in-depth knowledge about a model and its peculiarities, a well-suited indicator may be chosen. This proceeding requires lots of knowledge about a model itself as well as detailed knowledge about possible indicators. Bearing in mind that a model developer should not need in-depth knowledge about the simulation engine actually executing a model, this approach seems to be not feasible. Ideally, a simulation engine takes care of all aspects related with model execution, especially of executing a model in a most efficent way.

One possible approach is to apply methods and techniques of self-optimization. A simulation engine could use an uninformed partitioning strategy at the beginning and regularly update the partitioning. Of course, the easiest realization of self-optimization would use the indicators mentioned before (e. g., minimal network traffic). A more sophisticated approach could employ methods of genetic algorithms to create and update a partitioning, combined with an evaluation of the current partition based on the actual runtime. For this purpose, a simulation engine could measure the runtime for a while (e. g., 100 time steps), update the partitioning and continue with the simulation. Provided that a simulation is long enough, a good partitioning may be found after a while.

8.1.5 Partitioning strategies on cluster-level

Node-level parallelization assumes that it is possible to execute a model on a single computing node. In contrast, cluster-level parallelization allows to split and distribute a model across multiple computing nodes. Similar to node-level parallelization two approaches are possible:

- Only the set of agents is distributed onto available nodes. The environment is replicated on each node, i. e., each node contains information about the whole environment.

- Additionally to the set of agents, the environment is also split up and distributed onto available nodes.

Obviously, decomposing and distributing the simulated environment onto multiple computing nodes allows simulation of very large models. This is especially important if a model is too large to be executed on a single computing node.

The decomposition approaches described for node-level parallelization can also be applied to cluster-level parallelization. Four different combinations are distinguished:

- Static/ Agents only
  The environment is replicated onto all nodes. The static partitioning of the set of agents is uninformed as no specific information is taken into account (cp. static partitioning on node-level as described in Section 8.1.3).

- Static/ Agents and environment
  Depending on the type of environment, a decomposition into n partitions is computed. The set of agents is distributed onto the nodes according to the environmental decomposition. Both decompositions of environment and the set of agents are computed only once (static).

- Dynamic/ Agents only
  The environment is replicated onto all nodes. A dynamic partitioning of the agents may take additional information gathered during runtime into account, e. g., interaction pattern (cp. dynamic partitioning on node-level as described in Section 8.1.4).

- Dynamic/ Agents and environment
  Besides only taking into account additional information for computing the partitioning of the agents, the additional information gathered during a simulation is also taken into account to compute a decomposition of the environment. As described in Section 8.1.4 the benefits of a better decomposition have to be balanced against the resources required for computing and updating the partitioning.

Regarding multi-level parallelization each of the approaches applied on cluster-level may be combined with the approaches for node-level parallelization.

8.2 Parallel execution

As illustrated in Figure 8.1 parallel execution of an agent-based simulation is possible on different levels. Within this thesis three levels of parallelization are distinguished:

- Parallelization on cluster-level

- Parallelization on node-level

- Parallelization on processor-level

Although parallelization can be employed on these three levels, it is important to keep in mind that there is exactly one agent-based model which is executed. The execution is performed by a simulation engine which may be implemented in any fashion (e. g., as a distributed system).

Parallelization on cluster-level refers to executing a simulation engine on multiple interconnected computing nodes. Each component of a simulation engine running on a dedicated computing node may be parallelized further. *Node-level parallelization* refers to parallelizing the execution of a simulation engine on a single node, i. e., to use multiple processors of a computing node. *Processor-level parallelization* addresses the issue that each processor may contain multiple cores and therefore may execute multiple threads in parallel.

The combined application of parallelization strategies on different levels is called *Multi-Level Parallelization*. Similar terms which may be found in literature are nested parallelism [117] as well as hierarchical parallelism and multi-stage parallelism [82]. In the following, only the term *parallelization* is used.

As parallelization issues on processor- and node-level are very similar, these two levels are not treated independently. The two resulting parallelization level (cluster-level, node- and processor-level) are described in detail in the following subsections.

8.2.1 Parallelization on node- and processor-level

Parallelizing the execution of an agent-based simulation on node- and processor level refers to the multi-threaded execution of a simulation engine. As illustrated in Figure 8.1 node- and processor-level parallelization includes the usage of multiple processors within one computing node as well as exploiting multiple cores within a processor. Compared to a simulation engine running on multiple nodes, parallelization on node- and processor-level has a lot in common:

- Intra-node and intra-processor communication is orders of magnitudes faster than inter-node communication, which usually involves network connections. Besides pure bandwidth also latency and response times of intra-node and intra-processor communication are much smaller when compared to network connections.

- Intra-node and intra-processor communication is highly reliable. In contrast to network connections, there is no need to consider unreliable or unstable communication. Thus, sophisticated mechanisms and protocols to ensure integrity of communication are not necessary.

- Considering parallelization on node- and processor-level, a simulation engine (and all its threads) act on a single memory. Therefore, all communication and synchronization is handled via this shared memory.

With these properties in mind, the main challenge for parallelization on node- and processor-level is to devise synchronization strategies which ensure correctness, integrity and causality of a simulation and permit substantial parallel execution to achieve good speedup.

8.2.2 Parallelization on cluster-level

As illustrated in Figure 8.1, cluster-level parallelization refers to the execution of a simulation engine on multiple computing nodes. Major reasons for cluster-level parallelization are:

- Performance
  Employing cluster-level parallelization may be the only way to achieve performance speedups which are impossible to realize on a single computing node.

- Memory and model size
  Considering fairly large models, a single computing node may not have the required amount of memory necessary for executing a model. By splitting up a model and distributing it to multiple nodes, even very large models may be handled.

Compared to node- and processor-level parallelization, the main differences are the limitations imposed by network connections between the nodes. This includes lower bandwidth, reduced speed, increased latency and response times as well as the fact that network communication between nodes can not be assumed to be reliable.

A simulation engine realizing cluster-level parallelization may be implemented in various ways, e. g., with a central control node or in a completely decentralized manner.

8.2.3 Multi-level parallelization

Multi-level parallelization refers to the simultaneous use of node- and processor level parallelization and cluster-level parallelization. First, a simulation engine may use multiple nodes; thus the model is partitioned accordingly. Second, for each node a simulation engine may further parallelize execution and use multiple processors and threads. Obviously, model partitioning and parallelization of a simulation engine are tightly related and have to go hand in hand.

8.3 Reliability of a simulation environment

Besides improving performance (i. e., reducing runtime) parallelization may also be used for increasing reliability. The underlying computing hardware is utilized by a simulation engine and *invisible* for the actual model that is executed. Instead of using all available resources for achieving maximum speedup, a simulation engine might exploit some hardware resources for increasing reliability of the simulation environment.

The importance of reliability increases with the amount of hardware resources utilized by a simulation engine. Therefore, especially if huge computing systems are considered (e. g., containing hundreds of processors) dealing with reliability is essential. In the same way as a simulation engine can use available hardware resources for performance reasons, a simulation engine may as well utilize a portion of the resources for reliability issues.

The actual strategies of a simulation engine for improving reliability may be very different. Possible options include introducing redundancy as well as providing fault-detection and fault-correction mechanisms (cp. [49]).

9 Example implementation of GRAMS

The GRAMS reference model is a conceptual reference model and as such it aims primarily at the development of conceptual models. For demonstrating the practical applicability of the GRAMS reference model, an example implementation is developed which is presented in this chapter.

9.1 Overview

According to the model development process as described in Section 2.1.3 the example implementation is settled at the level of the executable model and serves the following purposes:

- Demonstrate applicability of the GRAMS reference model (*proof-of-concept*)
  - to develop agent-based models and
  - to serve as a guideline for implementing different simulation engines.

- Provide a baseline for comparing different simulation engines (in this thesis, especially sequential and parallel simulation engines).

The example implementation is developed from scratch and does not make use of frameworks or tools like JAMES II [57] and Repast [4]. Although it should be possible to represent the GRAMS reference model within these frameworks and tools, the decision was not to use any of the available frameworks and tools. Developing the example

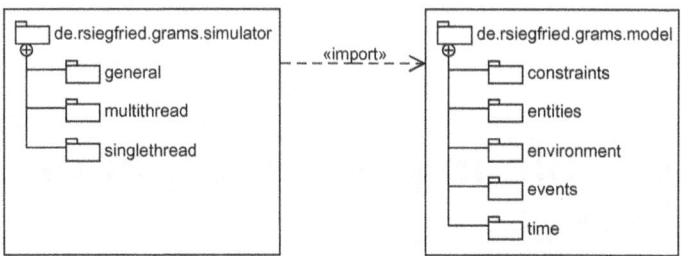

Figure 9.1: Package structure of example implementation.

implementation from scratch opens up all possibilities and allows a very concise implementation. The example implementation resembles the GRAMS reference model very closely without the need to take into account additional ideas or constraints from a framework or tool. Of course, mature frameworks and tools (like JAMES II and Repast) offer many benefits like experiment design or result analysis which are not included in the example implementation of the GRAMS reference model. This is not considered a disadvantage as the example implementation is used solely for the purposes outlined above, and is not intended to be or to become a production grade software system.

Like the GRAMS reference model itself, the example implementation consists of two major parts (see package diagram shown in Figure 9.1):

- Representation of an agent-based model.
  The package `de.rsiegfried.grams.model` of the example implementation provides interfaces and abstract classes which serve as basis for developing problem-specific models and are reusable across all problem-specific models.

- Implementation of simulation engines.
  The package `de.rsiegfried.grams.simulator` contains the implementations of different simulation engines. Although many different simulation engines are conceivable, all simulation engines operate solely on the problem-independent interfaces and abstract classes defined in the `model`-package.

When it comes to the actual implementation, the following two questions need to be answered:

1. Which language shall be used for representing a model itself?
   Within this question the general decision has to be made whether to use a domain-specific modeling language (e. g., FABLES [50], ELMS [96]) or a general purpose programming language to represent an agent-based model.

2. Which programming language shall be used for implementing simulation engines?
   This question may have multiple answers, as different simulation engines may be implemented in different programming languages. The only requirement is that all simulation engines execute the given agent-based models.

In the course of this thesis, Java was chosen as both the language for representing models as well as for implementing simulation engines. This choice is mainly based on the following two facts (cp. [117]). Firstly, as an object-oriented language, Java is well-suited to represent agent-based models. Using an object-oriented language helps to minimize the semantic distance of the implementation to the reference model in a very natural fashion (see [60, p. 286], [88]). Secondly, Java offers built-in support for multi-threading. Therefore it is suitable for implementing multi-threaded simulation engines without the need for additional tools or languages.

As illustrated in Figure 9.1, the example implementation follows the reference model very closely. Especially, no new terms are introduced but the terms of the GRAMS reference model are used whereever possible without introducing ambiguities. In the following, the representation of an agent-based model is presented exactly in the same order as the GRAMS reference model is presented in Chapter 6. Afterwards the implementation of simulation engines is described.

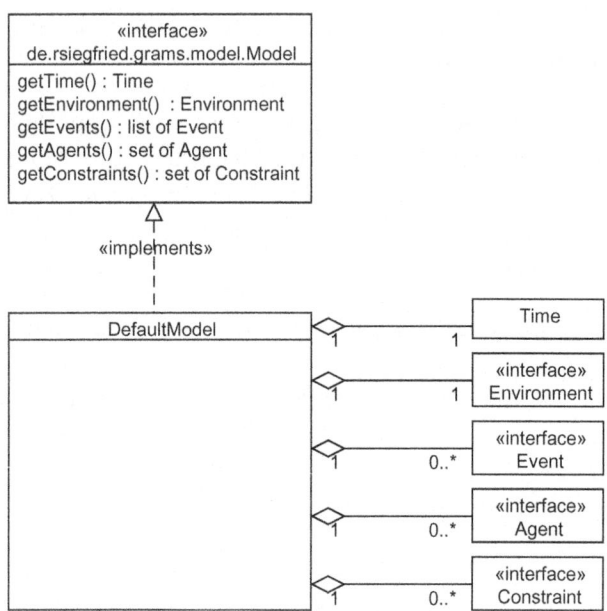

Figure 9.2: Main classes and interfaces representing an agent-based model.

9.2 Representation of an agent-based model

The right-hand side of Figure 9.1 already indicates that agent-based models as defined by the GRAMS reference model are represented in a very direct way. The package `grams.model` serves as top-level package and contains all sub-packages and classes. In a very straight-forward way, the sub-packages `time`, `environment`, `events`, `entities` and `constraints` contain the respective concepts.

The package `grams.model` furthermore contains the interface `Model` which provides access to the components of an agent-based model. As indicated in Figure 9.2, default implementations of interfaces are regularly provided to ease implementation of problem-specific models. Details of individual classes and interfaces are provided in the following subsections.

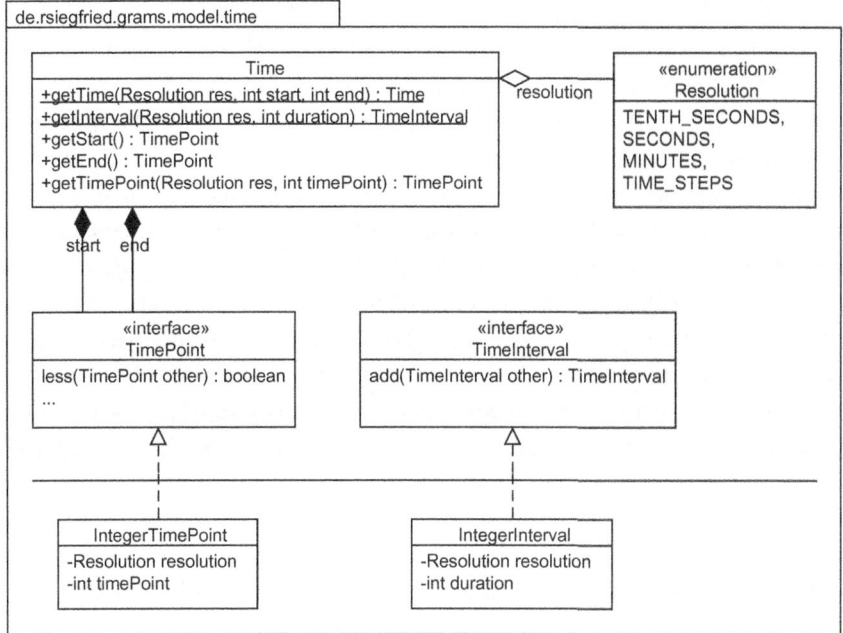

Figure 9.3: Class diagram of package time.

9.2.1 Simulation time

The simulation time is represented by the class Time and the two interfaces TimePoint and TimeInterval (see Figure 9.3). Furthermore, due to the discretization of simulation time, the enumeration type Resolution is introduced.

The central class of this package is Time. In order to create an instance of this class, the client has to call the static getTime()-method. This method takes as arguments the desired resolution as well as the start point and end point of the simulation time. The start point and end point are evaluated by the simulation engine and define the duration (in terms of simulation time) of a simulation.

The interfaces TimePoint and TimeInterval define operations available on a single point in time and on a time interval (e. g., comparison operators needed to establish total ordering of points in time). As objects of these interfaces may only be created via the getTimePoint()- and getInterval()-methods of class Time, each point in time and each time interval is defined with respect to the previously specified resolution.

Time points as well as time intervals may be implemented in various ways. Figure 9.3 depicts a solution which uses integer values to store time points and duration of time intervals. The number of time points is therefore limited by the domain of the integer data type (in Java, int ranges from -2^{31} to $2^{31} - 1$ [47, § 4.2.1]) and accordingly the maximum simulation time is given by the maximum number of time points and the chosen resolution. The same reasoning applies for time intervals. It has to be noted that all clients only work with the public interfaces TimePoint and TimeInterval; the actual implementations (in this case IntegerTimePoint and IntegerInterval) are not publicly accessable.

The enumeration type Resolution defines the possible resolutions which may be used. On the one hand common resolutions like seconds, minutes, etc. are supported, but on the other hand, artificial resolutions like time steps (which have no direct relation to real world time units) are also supported. Within one model, only compatible resolutions may be used. This requirement is currently not enforced by the example implementation, but left to the responsibility of the developer.

9.2.2 Environment

As depicted in Figure 9.4 the environment is represented by the three interfaces Environment, Location and Coordinate. Whereas Environment and Location directly reflect the corresponding concepts of the GRAMS reference model (see Section 6.4.2), the interface Coordinate is introduced to specify locations using a specific coordinate system. All three interfaces may be implemented in various ways (e. g., GridEnvironment, ContinuousEnvironment), Figure 9.4 shows Coordinate2D as a representation of a simple 2-dimensional coordinate system.

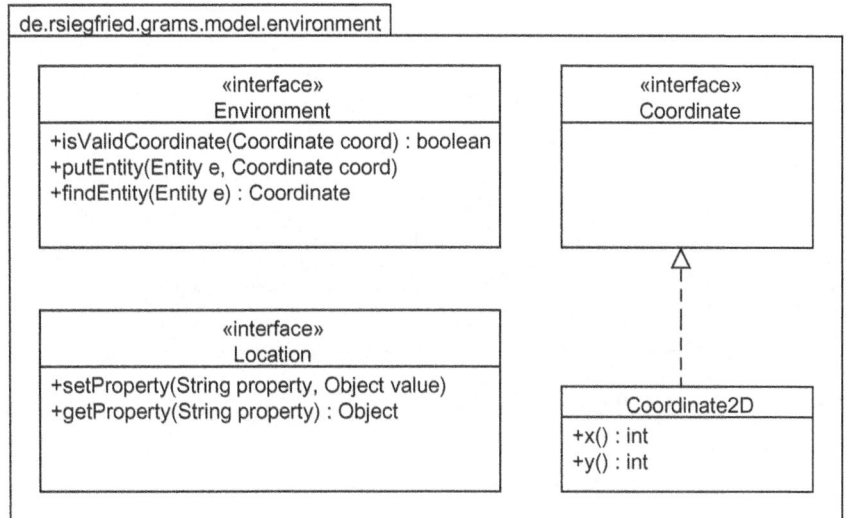

Figure 9.4: Class diagram of package `environment`.

The integration of environmental update functions is not explicitly depicted in Figure 9.4. Currently, environmental update functions are treated very much the same way as actions of agents: Each update function is triggered by an event and has a specific duration during which it changes affected locations.

9.2.3 Events

Figure 9.5 illustrates the representation of events within the example implementation. As all events occur at a specific point in time, all event types have to implement the interface Event. On the implementation-side only two different types of events are distinguished on the highest level:

- EnvironmentalEvent represents events occuring in the model environment and affecting either the environment or some entities embedded in it. This type of events corresponds to the event categories numbered (1) and (2) in Figure 6.5.

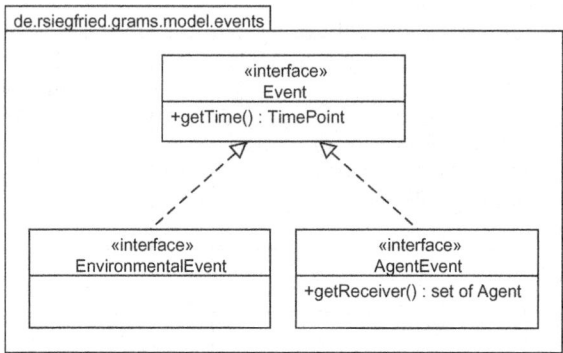

Figure 9.5: Class diagram of package events.

- AgentEvent represents all types of events which directly influence one or more agents. This type of events corresponds to the event categories numbered (2) and (3) in Figure 6.5.

It should be mentioned once more that these events are parts of the agent-based model itself and do not impose any specific execution paradigm of actual simulation engines. Especially, these events have to be distinguished from the so-called *simulator events* in Section 9.3.1 which are introduced solely for purposes of execution control.

9.2.4 Constraints

The representation of constraints is straight-forward (see Figure 9.6). A single constraint is defined by the interface **Constraint**, a set of constraints by the interface **Constraints**. Both, a single constraint as well as a set of constraints, provide a method for evaluating the constraint respectively set of constraints which directly reflects the definition of the GRAMS reference model (see Section 6.6.4).

Evaluation is the abstract base class for representing the result of evaluating a constraint, respectively a set of constraints. Currently four different evaluation results are distinguished:

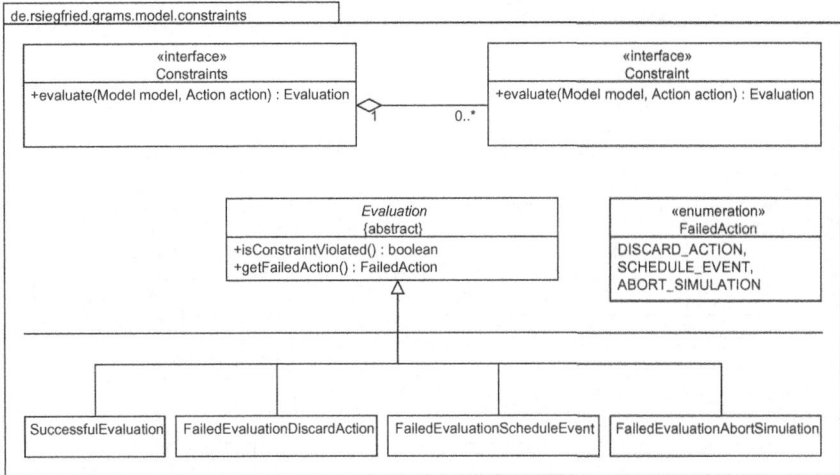

Figure 9.6: Class diagram of package `constraints`.

- **SuccessfulEvaluation**
  Indicates that the constraint(s) were evaluated successfully.

- **FailedEvaluationScheduleEvent**
  Indicates that at least one constraint is violated, i. e., the evaluation failed. As response to this constraint violation, an event shall be scheduled.

  Example: A constraint could be that no more than one agent is at the same position. If two agents try to move to the same location at the same time, a collision-event is scheduled.

- **FailedEvaluationDiscardAction**
  Indicates that at least one constraint is violated, i. e., the evaluation failed. As response to this constraint violation, the action shall be discarded. In this case, the simulation engine cancels the execution of the specified action immediately.

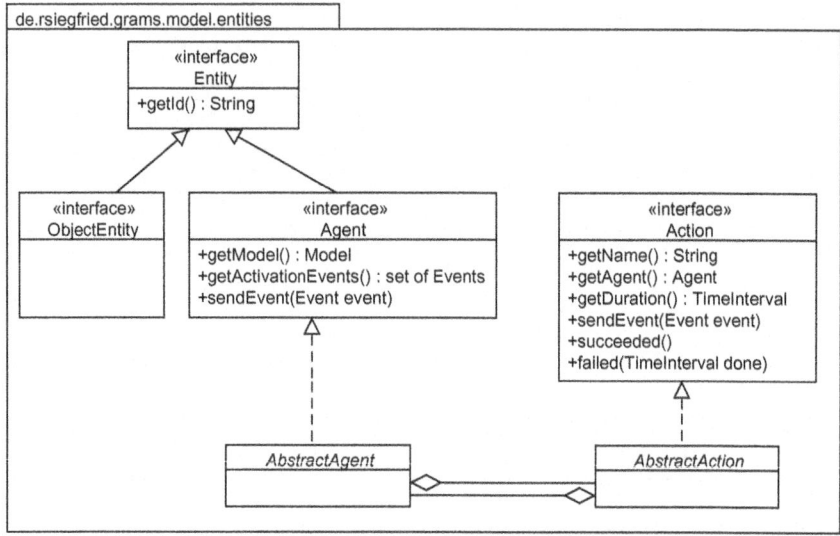

Figure 9.7: Class diagram of package `entities`.

- FailedEvaluationAbortSimulation

  Indicates that at least one constraint is violated, i. e., the evaluation
  failed. As response to this constraint violation, the simulation shall
  be aborted. This response may be very helpful during development
  or if a constraint is violated in a way that simulation results would
  not be valid any longer.

The client only copes with the abstract class **Evaluation** and the
enumeration type **FailedAction**, the actual implementations are not
visible to the client.

9.2.5 Entities

Entities, i. e., objects and agents, are represented as shown in Figure 9.7. Both, sensors and effectors of an agent, are represented by
the interface **Action**. In addition to the GRAMS reference model, each
agent and also each action has a unique identifier.

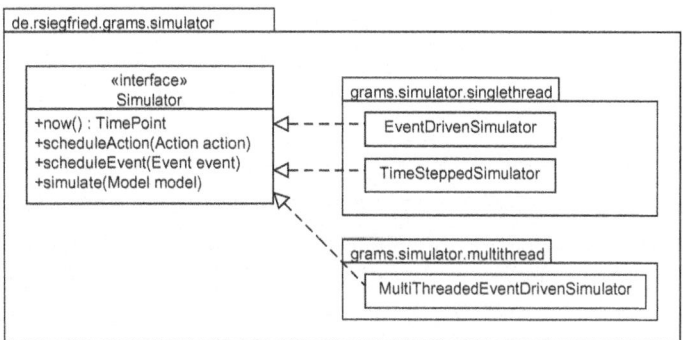

Figure 9.8: Class diagram of package `simulator`.

Actual classes implementing the interface **Agent** represent the different types of agents available in problem-specific models. The class **AbstractAgent** provides a skeletal implementation of an agent to ease implementation.

Two methods of an action are worth mentioning:

- `succeeded()`

  This method is called by a simulation engine if the execution of this action was successfully. In this case, this method is responsible for determining the state changes which have to be applied to the model.

- `failed(TimeInterval done)`

  This method is called by a simulation engine and indicates that the execution of this action failed after the amount of time specified by the parameter **done**. Similarly to the case of a successful execution, this method is responsible for determining the state changes which have to be applied to the model.

9.3 Simulation engines

The starting point for implementing a simulation engine is the interface **Simulator** (see Figure 9.8). Two different single-threaded implement-

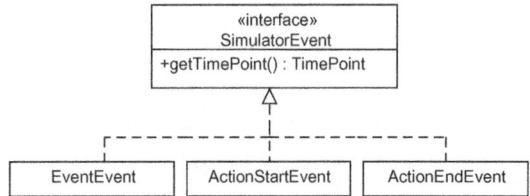

Figure 9.9: Class diagram of *simulator events* used by event-driven simulation engines.

ations as well as a multi-threaded implementation of a simulation engine are shown in Figure 9.8. Even if a simulation engine is realized as a distributed system it appears to the user as a single system providing the rather simple interface **Simulator**.

9.3.1 Single-threaded event-driven simulation engine

A single-threaded event-driven simulation engine possesses two main characteristics:

- The simulation engine is *single-threaded*, i. e., it makes no use of eventually possible execution of multiple threads at the same time.

- The simulation engine is *event-driven*, i. e., the simulation is always advanced to the point in time when the next event happens without considering the time in between.

Given these two main characteristics, this simulation engine is considered the easiest possible implementation of a simulation engine adhering to the definitions of the GRAMS reference model.

As already mentioned in Section 6.5, it is important to distinguish precisely between two different types of events: In the first case, *events* are part of a model (see Section 6.5). The second type of events, *simulator events*, is used by a simulation engine for controlling the execution of a simulation. Figure 9.9 shows the simulator events used by this event-driven simulation engine. The following mapping is used from events and actions of a model to simulator events:

Agent-based model	Simulation engine (implementation)
Event	EventEvent
Action	ActionStartEvent × ActionEndEvent

This means, each model event is mapped onto a corresponding simulator event. Each action of an agent (either sensor or effector action) is mapped onto two simulator events, namely one for the start of an action and one for the end of an action.

Algorithm 2 Main loop of the single-threaded event-driven simulation engine

---

futureEvents = [*0 : StartEvent*]
now = timeOfFirstEvent(futureEvents)
while futureEvents not empty AND now ¡ end **do**
    now = timeOfFirstEvent(futureEvents)
    currentEvents = futureEvents.eventsAt(now)
    for all ActionEndEvent *e* in currentEvents **do**
        The action corresponding to event *e* could be executed successfully, therefore change model state accordingly
    end for
    for all EnvironmentalEvent *e* in currentEvents **do**
        Update environment and check constraints
    end for
    for all AgentEvent *e* in currentEvents **do**
        Relay event *e* to agents
    end for
    for all ActionStartEvent *e* in currentEvents **do**
        Check constraints AND handle violated constraints
    end for
end while

The main loop of the event-driven simulation engine is shown in Algorithm 2. The `futureEvents` data structure holds all upcoming events (timepoint and event). At the beginning, `futureEvents` is initialized to hold the StartEvent which is sent to all agents at the beginning of a simulation. Each agent will relay the received **StartEvent** to all of its sensors and effectors susceptible for this kind of event. Depending on the actual behavior implemented in the agents, they will start *living*.

The variable **now** always holds the current simulation time and is advanced to the point in time of the next event each time the simulation loop is executed. After updating the variable **currentEvents** to contain all simulator events which occur at the current point in time, the events are processed in the following order: First, successfully finished actions are executed. Secondly, the events are processed; both the events which influence only the environment (type (1)) and those which directly influence agents (type (2)). Finally, actions which start at the current point in time are processed.

The constraints are checked when an environmental event occurs and at the beginning of an action. As these are the two only points when an action may either fail (due to a modified environment) or interfere with another action, it is sufficient to evaluate constraints at these points in time.

9.3.2 Single-threaded time-stepped simulation engine

This section describes briefly the implementation of a second simulation engine which realizes a time-stepped execution. The time increment per step may be chosen arbitrarily as long as it is sufficient small, i. e., at least small enough to schedule all simulator events.

As expected, Algorithm 3 is very much the same as Algorithm 2. Actually, the main difference is that simulation time progresses just a small amount Δ in each simulation cycle. The processing of actions and events as well as checking of constraints is handled completely the same way in both simulation engines.

Unlike the event-driven simulation engine, the time-stepped simulation engine may compute changes in the environment (e. g., by environmental update functions) or the embedding (e. g., movement of an agent) in each step. This may help to avoid typical artifacts of

---

Algorithm 3 Main loop of the single-threaded time-stepped simulation engine

---

futureEvents $= [0 : StartEvent]$
now $= 0$
while now ¡ end **do**
  currentEvents $=$ futureEvents.eventsAt(now)
  for all ActionEndEvent e in currentEvents **do**
    The action corresponding to event e could be executed successfully, therefore change model state accordingly
  end for
  for all EnvironmentalEvent e in currentEvents **do**
    Update environment and check constraints
  end for
  for all AgentEvent e in currentEvents **do**
    Relay event e to agents
  end for
  for all ActionStartEvent e in currentEvents **do**
    check constraints AND handle violated constraints
  end for
  now $=$ now $+ \Delta$
end while

---

event-driven simulation (like 'jumping' entities) which is often required for visualizing simulations in a realistic and appealing manner.

9.3.3 Parallelization on node-level

This section presents the extension of the example implementation with respect to parallel execution. The simulation engine described in this section demonstrates the feasibility of the approach proposed by this thesis: The agent-based model itself needs to be developed just once and may be executed by various simulation engines producing identical results, but possibly making use of parallel execution.

Some changes of technical nature to a model are necessary and
concern specific synchronization issues which are partially introduced
by the chosen programming language. This situation is pointed out
excellently by Brian Götz et al.:

> 'When concurrency is introduced into an application by
> a framework, it is usually impossible to restrict the con-
> currency-awareness to the framework code, because frame-
> works by their nature make callbacks to application com-
> ponents that in turn access application state.' [45, p. 9]

First of all, implementation of node-level partitioning strategies requires the representation of model partitions. The interface Partition
defines a basic set of operations for creating and updating partitions of
a set of agents. Figure 9.10 gives an overview of the extended package
diagram containing the simulation engines as well as additionally
required interfaces and classes.

The Partition-interface resembles closely the approach specified in
Section 8.1.4. The class AgentStatic realizes the uninformed node-
level partitioning strategy as described in Section 8.1.3 (i. e., static
partitioning on a per-agent basis). Given a set of agents and a set
of execution threads, this partitioning strategy does not take any
information into account. The agents are distributed randomly and
uniformly onto the available execution threads.

Using static partitioning strategies

The adaptation of the event-driven simulation engine is shown in
Algorithm 4 (shaded area highlight differences to single-threaded
simulation engine). As a great amount of computation occurs when an
action is executed successfully (namely, the associated state changes),
only this part of the algorithm is actually executed in parallel. This
partitioning strategy ensures that state changes related to successful
execution of a number of actions are computed in parallel.

Synchronization is straight-forward to handle in this case: Only if an
action is executed successfully (see Chapter 6.6.5), the corresponding

Algorithm 4 Multi-threaded event-driven simulation engine using a *node-level/per agent/static* partitioning strategy.

partition = uninformed($\mathbb{A}, T$) // see Algorithm 1

futureEvents = [*0 : StartEvent*]
now = timeOfFirstEvent(futureEvents)
while futureEvents not empty AND now ¡ end **do**
   now = timeOfFirstEvent(futureEvents)
   currentEvents = futureEvents.eventsAt(now)

      for all ActionEndEvent *e* in currentEvents **do**
         Action *x* of agent *A* corresponding to event *e* is executed
         successfully
         Use thread *t* = partition(*A*) for computing corresponding
         state changes
      end for

   for all EnvironmentalEvent *e* in currentEvents **do**
      Update environment and check constraints
   end for
   for all AgentEvent *e* in currentEvents **do**
      Relay event *e* to agents
   end for
   for all ActionStartEvent *e* in currentEvents **do**
      check constraints AND handle violated constraints
   end for
end while

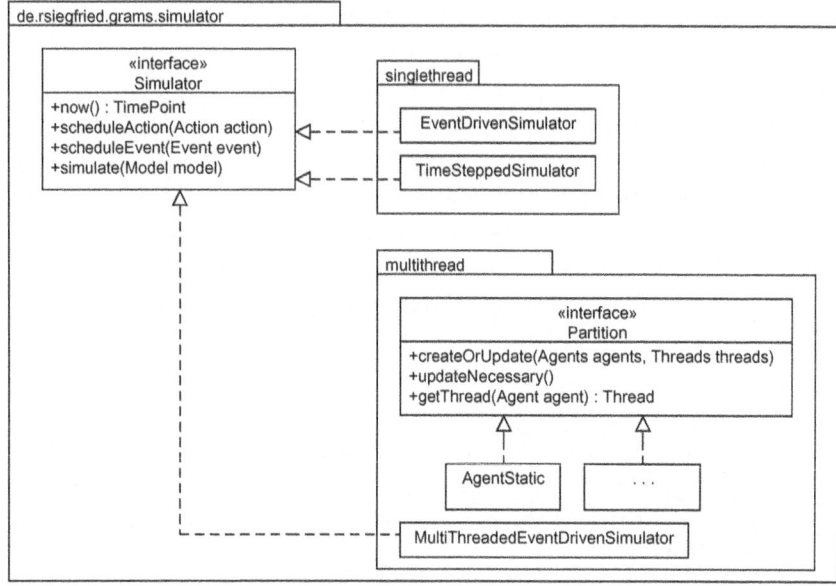

Figure 9.10: Class diagram of package `simulator` with partitioning support.

ActionEndEvent is triggered. Successful execution of an action implies that this action does not conflict with any other action, therefore state changes associated with this action are independent of all other actions. Due to this independence, there is no need for special synchronization. Of course, within the actual implementation concurrent access on shared resources (e. g., a list) has to be synchronized.

Using dynamic partitioning strategies

The basic adaptations to a simulation engine for exploiting a dynamic partitioning strategy are illustrated in Algorithm 5 (shaded area highlight differences to single-threaded simulation engine). Firstly, the actually used partitioning strategy s has to be specified. The additional context information needed for computing the partitioning (e. g., maximum affected area by an action) is not denoted expli-

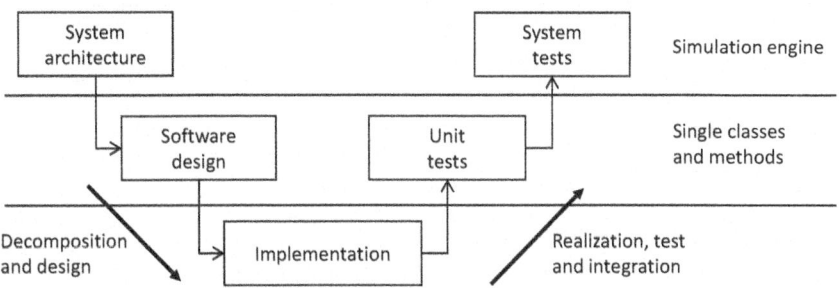

Figure 9.11: Development of the example implementation follows a simplified V-Model.

citly, but indicated via the function name `informed()` (instead of `uninformed()`).

9.3.4 Parallelization on cluster-level

Considering parallelization on cluster-level the implementation of a simulation engine is considerably more complex. This is largely due to the fact that any simulation engine which employs cluster-level parallelization is a decentralized software system with all its benefits and pitfalls. The most important choice to make when implementing such a simulation engine is to decide whether a central control node exists or not. On the one hand, a central control node simplifies many aspects (e. g., management issues like starting and stopping a simulation and collecting simulation results). On the other hand, a central control node may easily become a bottleneck and thus limit optimal performance speedups.

9.4 Test and verification

As one of the main intentions of the example implementation is to provide a reference (i. e., to serve as a guideline for implementing simulation engines), the example implementation follows the GRAMS reference model closely. Development of the example implementation

Algorithm 5 Multi-threaded event-driven simulation engine using a *node-level/per agent/dynamic* partitioning strategy.

Require: Use partitioning strategy s
  partition = informed($\mathbb{A}, T, s, \emptyset$)

futureEvents = [$0 : StartEvent$]
now = timeOfFirstEvent(futureEvents)
while futureEvents not empty AND now ¡ end **do**
  now = timeOfFirstEvent(futureEvents)
  currentEvents = futureEvents.eventsAt(now)

  for all ActionEndEvent e in currentEvents **do**
    Action x of agent A corresponding to event e is executed successfully
    Use thread t = partition(A) for computing corresponding state changes
  end for

  for all EnvironmentalEvent e in currentEvents **do**
    Update environment and check constraints
  end for
  for all AgentEvent e in currentEvents **do**
    Relay event e to agents
  end for
  for all ActionStartEvent e in currentEvents **do**
    check constraints (using additional information) AND handle violated constraints
  end for

  if partitionUpdateNecessary() **then**
    partition = informed($\mathbb{A}, T, s$, partition)
  end if

end while

is guided by a V-model as shown in Figure 9.11 (cp. [102, p. 16ff.], [92, p. 106ff.]).

The correctness of each individual class of the example implementation is verified by unit tests (also known as module tests or component tests). By definition, a unit is the smallest testable part of an application. Therefore, the unit tests designed for the example implementation cover only a single method at a time. Although the invocation of a single method will usually trigger secondary method invocations, the objective of a single unit test case is to test only exactly one method. Additionally, by definition unit testing only tests the functionality of units themselves and will not catch integration errors, or broader system level errors (such as functions performed across multiple units, or non-functional test areas such as performance).

Whereas the V-model usually proposes a 4-step approach of integration (unit tests, integration tests, system tests and acceptance tests), development and test of the example implementation follows a tailored 2-step approach. Unit tests are used extensively to ensure correct functionality of single modules. All unit tests (326 tests, test coverage of packages varies between 42 and 97 %) passed successfully.

The subsequent integration and system tests to ensure correct functionality of multiple units and the whole simulation engine are combined into a single test step. The reason for this is that integration tests are simply not necessary as the system as a whole is not that complex and big. Separately defining and executing these kinds of tests seems not to improve test coverage. As shown in Figure 9.11 the system tests address the whole simulation engine. The system tests are based on a Tileworld-model (see following section for model details) and verify the conformance of a specific implementation of a simulation engine with the definitions of the GRAMS reference model.

Actually, the system tests ensure that the state trajectories produced by the presented simulation engines are identical. Instead of only testing the equality of the final states produced by the simulation engines, the system tests check whether all states of a simulation produced by the simulation engines are identical. As expected the simulation engines deliver identical simulation results when simulating the same model.

9.5 Empirical measurements

This section provides empirical measurements of several key performance metrics. The runtime behavior of a simulation of an agent-based model according to the GRAMS reference model is analyzed by several benchmark suites. The primary metric used to measure performance is the runtime which denotes the amount of computing time necessary for executing a single simulation. A secondary metric is the amount of *memory* used in total by each simulation engine to execute a single simulation of a model.

All benchmarks are based on the Tileworld-model as described in the next subsection. The following computing infrastructure was used:

- Processor: Intel Core i5-650 (4-core processor)

- Memory: 4 GB

- Software: Windows 7 (64 Bit), Jave Runtime Environment 1.6.20 (32 bit edition)

In the following subsections, the Tileworld-Model and the various benchmark suites are described, the results are presented and an interpretation of the results is given.

9.5.1 Simulation model used for benchmarks

The simulation model used for all benchmarks is adapted from the Tileworld-model [103]. This section describes the simulation model according to the GRAMS reference model.

Macro-level: Simulation time

As simulation time a discrete time domain is chosen, i. e., $\mathbb{T} = \mathbb{N} = \{0, 1, 2, \ldots t_{\max}\}$. The simulation time has no direct relation to real

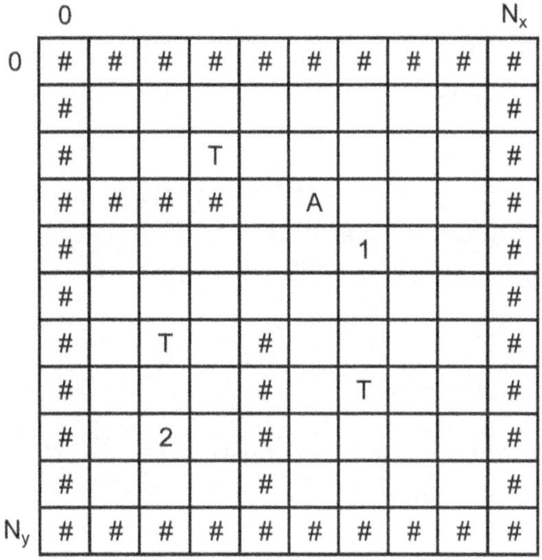

	0									N_x
0	#	#	#	#	#	#	#	#	#	#
	#									#
	#			T						#
	#	#	#	#		A				#
	#					1				#
	#									#
	#		T		#					#
	#				#	T				#
	#		2		#					#
	#				#					#
N_y	#	#	#	#	#	#	#	#	#	#

Figure 9.12: Schematics of the Tileworld environment (A = agent, # = obstacle, T = tile, *digit* = hole).

time, i. e., a conversion from simulation time (time steps) into real time (seconds, minutes, etc.) is not defined in a meaningful manner.

Macro-level: Environment

The Tileworld environment is modeled as rectangular grid of equal-sized cells (see Figure 9.12). Each cell is uniquely identified by its (x, y)-coordinates, with the origin $(0, 0)$ being in the upper-left corner. The environment extends from 0 to N_x in horizontal direction, and from 0 to N_y in vertical direction. Therefore, the size of the environment is $(N_x + 1) \times (N_y + 1)$ cells.

The cells of the environment are distinguished into three different types:

- *Normal* area
  No speciality. Agents may walk here.

- Obstacles
  Obstacles limit the agents movement as agents cannot move onto
  cells of this type. Obstacles can not be moved or destroyed.

- Holes
  Holes designate target areas for tiles. Each hole h has a specific
  capacity $C_h^{\max}$ and a current fill level C_h. Agents may put tiles into
  a hole as long as its current fill level does not exceed its capacity,
  i. e., as long as $C_h < C_h^{\max}$.

Macro-level: Constraints

The simulation model defines no constraints, nevertheless individual
constraints may be defined separately by specific benchmarks.

Events

The following exogenous events may occur in the simulation:

- *Start*-Event
  Special event denoting the start of a simulation. This event is sent
  to all agents at the beginning of a simulation.

- *TileCreation*-Event
  Events of this type can be pre-scheduled by a user and lead to
  creation of a tile at a specific location at a deterministic point in
  time.

Additionally, endogenous events within single agents may occur.

Micro-level: Tiles

Tiles are the object of desire of the agents. Tiles do not have any
attributes. They are available on normal area and may be carried by
agents to holes.

Micro-level: Agent

A Tileworld-agent is characterized by the following attributes:

- environment

- current position: $(x, y) \in (0 \leq N_x, 0 \leq N_y)$

- current target: $(x, y) \in (0 \leq N_x, 0 \leq N_y)$

- tile: yes/no (indicates whether the agent is currently carrying a tile)

A Tileworld-agent has just a *Perceive*-sensor. With this sensor, the agent may perceive the status of the environment. Each perceive-action takes 1 time step and perfect perception is assumed, i.e., all obstacles, tiles and holes are identified correctly. Furthermore, a Tileworld-agent is equipped with four effectors:

- The *Plan*-effector contains the planning process (i.e., selection of tiles and holes, path planning). Each plan-action takes 1 time step.

- The *Move*-effector is used for moving one step ahead (north, east, south, or west). Each move-action takes 1 time step.

- The *Pick-up*-effector is used to pick up tiles. In order to pick up a tile, an agent has to be on the same cell. Each pick-up-action takes 1 time step.

- The *Put-down*-effector is used to put a tile into a hole. In order to put a tile into a hole, an agent has to be on an adjacent cell (as agents may not walk on holes). Each put-down-action takes 1 time step.

Figure 9.13 illustrates the behavior of a Tileworld-agent. As soon as it perceives a tile, it starts moving to this tile. Once the tile is reached, it is picked up and the agent is headed for the closest hole. As soon as it arrives at the hole and is on a cell adjacent to the hole, it drops the tile into the hole. Afterwards, the agent is headed for the next tile. If no tile is present, the agent waits at his current position.

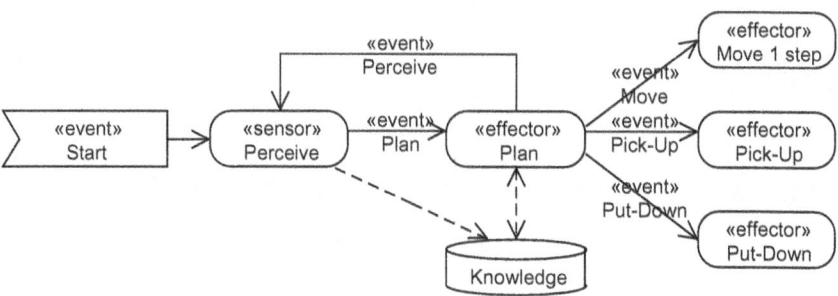

Figure 9.13: Sensor-effector-chains of the Tileworld-agent.

9.5.2 Benchmark suite 0: Dependency between simulation time and runtime

Benchmark suite 0 is intended to measure the dependency between simulation time and runtime. As argued in chapter 8.1.2, a simulation as defined by the GRAMS reference model only takes into account the current model state when computing a state change. Given a model of fixed size, runtime should scale linearly with elapsed simulation time.

Setup suite 0

All benchmarks in this suite operate on the same environment env03:

- Size: $1\,000 \times 1\,000$ cells

- $2\,000$ obstacles (randomly placed walls)

- $2\,000$ randomly placed tiles

- 100 randomly placed holes

This benchmark suite uses a single-threaded event-driven simulation engine. The test cases are documented in Table 9.1. The size of the model is fixed (environment, number of agents) and only the simulation time is varied.

Table 9.1: Setup of test cases for benchmark suite 0.

Test case	Nr of agents	Simulated time	Constraint?
TC_P_01	20	100 TIME STEPS	no
TC_P_02	20	200 TIME STEPS	no
TC_P_03	20	300 TIME STEPS	no
TC_P_04	20	400 TIME STEPS	no
TC_P_05	20	500 TIME STEPS	no
TC_P_06	20	1 000 TIME STEPS	no
TC_P_07	20	2 000 TIME STEPS	no
TC_P_01_b	20	100 TIME STEPS	yes
TC_P_02_b	20	200 TIME STEPS	yes
TC_P_03_b	20	300 TIME STEPS	yes
TC_P_04_b	20	400 TIME STEPS	yes
TC_P_05_b	20	500 TIME STEPS	yes
TC_P_06_b	20	1 000 TIME STEPS	yes
TC_P_07_b	20	2 000 TIME STEPS	yes

All test cases are specified in two versions. The first version of the test cases does not use any constraints. In contrast, the second version (indicated by the suffix '_b') uses a constraint. The constraint does not have any impact on the simulation results as it is just a dummy constraint to mimic the processing of constraints by a simulation engine.

Results, analysis and interpretation

The results of benchmark suite 0 are shown in Table 9.2. Each test case was executed 20 times. As expected, runtime scales linearly with elapsed simulation time. In this setup with up 20 agents, no significant runtime differences are observed due to constraint evaluation.

Table 9.2: Results of test cases for benchmark suite 0 (20 runs of each
test case).

Test case	Simulated time	Tiles	Runtime in seconds			Runtime (normalized)
			Avg	Min	Max	
TC_P_01	100	0	36.71	36.08	37.38	1.00
TC_P_02	200	37	71.32	70.50	72.46	1.94
TC_P_03	300	60	107.87	106.57	109.56	2.94
TC_P_04	400	80	144.56	142.12	146.29	3.94
TC_P_05	500	94	182.25	180.48	184.12	4.96
TC_P_06	1 000	181	373.23	368.55	377.47	10.17
TC_P_07	2 000	322	808.42	794.10	817.77	22.02
TC_P_01_b	100	0	36.70	36.28	36.99	1.00
TC_P_02_b	200	37	71.30	70.00	72.07	1.94
TC_P_03_b	300	60	108.19	106.96	110.24	2.95
TC_P_04_b	400	80	144.29	141.46	146.96	3.93
TC_P_05_b	500	94	182.53	178.71	185.19	4.97
TC_P_06_b	1 000	181	373.72	369.49	379.49	10.24
TC_P_07_b	2 000	322	813.31	800.02	821.40	22.16

9.5.3 Benchmark suites 1 and 2: Dependency between number of agents and runtime

The benchmark suites 1 and 2 are intended to measure the dependency
between number of agents and runtime. Whereas suite 1 uses smaller
numbers of agents (up to 200, see Table 9.3), suite 2 uses up to 10 000
agents (see Table 9.4).

As argued in chapter 8.1.2, runtime should scale quadratic with the
number of agents (due to constraint evaluation). In order to show the
influence of constraint evaluation both suites are defined without a
constraint and with a dummy constraint (indicated by the suffix '_b').

Setup suite 1

All benchmarks in suite 1 operate on the same environment env04:

- Size: 1 000 × 1 000 cells

Table 9.3: Setup of test cases for benchmark suite 1.

Test case	Simulated time	Nr of agents	Constraint?
TC_P_11	100 TIME STEPS	10	no
TC_P_12	100 TIME STEPS	20	no
TC_P_13	100 TIME STEPS	30	no
TC_P_14	100 TIME STEPS	40	no
TC_P_15	100 TIME STEPS	50	no
TC_P_16	100 TIME STEPS	100	no
TC_P_17	100 TIME STEPS	200	no
TC_P_11_b	100 TIME STEPS	10	yes
TC_P_12_b	100 TIME STEPS	20	yes
TC_P_13_b	100 TIME STEPS	30	yes
TC_P_14_b	100 TIME STEPS	40	yes
TC_P_15_b	100 TIME STEPS	50	yes
TC_P_16_b	100 TIME STEPS	100	yes
TC_P_17_b	100 TIME STEPS	200	yes

- 2 000 obstacles (randomly placed walls)

- 4 000 randomly placed tiles

- 100 randomly placed holes

This benchmark suite uses a single-threaded event-driven simulation engine. The test cases are documented in Table 9.3. The simulation time and the environment are fixed, the only parameter being varied is the number of agents.

Setup suite 2

In contrast to suite 1, suite 2 deals with lot larger numbers of agents. Therefore, this suite uses a significantly larger environment as well as a larger number of tiles and holes. All benchmarks in suite 2 operate on the same environment env05:

Table 9.4: Setup of test cases for benchmark suite 2.

Test case	Simulated time	Nr of agents	Constraint?
TC_P_21	100 TIME STEPS	1 000	no
TC_P_22	100 TIME STEPS	2 000	no
TC_P_23	100 TIME STEPS	3 000	no
TC_P_24	100 TIME STEPS	4 000	no
TC_P_25	100 TIME STEPS	5 000	no
TC_P_26	100 TIME STEPS	10 000	no
TC_P_21_b	100 TIME STEPS	1 000	yes
TC_P_22_b	100 TIME STEPS	2 000	yes
TC_P_23_b	100 TIME STEPS	3 000	yes
TC_P_24_b	100 TIME STEPS	4 000	yes
TC_P_25_b	100 TIME STEPS	5 000	yes
TC_P_26_b	100 TIME STEPS	10 000	yes

- Size: 1 500 × 1 500 cells

- 20 000 obstacles (randomly placed walls)

- 40 000 randomly placed tiles

- 1 500 randomly placed holes

This benchmark suite uses a single-threaded event-driven simulation engine. The test cases are documented in Table 9.4. The simulation time and the environment are fixed, the only parameter being varied is the number of agents.

Results, analysis and interpretation of benchmark suites 1 and 2

The results of benchmark suites 1 and 2 are shown in Table 9.5. In suite 1 no significant differences between test cases without and with constraint are observed. However, the runtime of test cases with constraint is slightly higher than for test cases without constraint.

Table 9.5: Results of test cases for benchmark suite 1 (20 runs of each
test case) and suite 2 (3 runs of each test case).

Test case	Nr of agents	Tiles	Runtime in seconds			Runtime (normalized)
			Avg	Min	Max	
TC_P_11	10	3	19.90	19.52	20.30	1.00
TC_P_12	20	13	40.65	39.78	41.17	2.04
TC_P_13	30	18	66.09	36.96	67.00	3.32
TC_P_14	40	22	90.28	89.61	91.29	4.54
TC_P_15	50	27	107.45	105.46	108.89	5.40
TC_P_16	100	60	215.61	211.82	219.29	10.84
TC_P_17	200	111	439.96	434.47	446.10	22.11
TC_P_11_b	10	3	19.80	19.61	20.03	1.00
TC_P_12_b	20	13	40.65	40.18	41.13	2.05
TC_P_13_b	30	18	65.98	65.33	66.68	3.33
TC_P_14_b	40	22	90.15	89.05	91.13	4.55
TC_P_15_b	50	27	108.02	106.72	109.93	5.45
TC_P_16_b	100	60	217.51	215.41	220.25	10.98
TC_P_17_b	200	111	451.64	445.46	456.23	22.81
TC_P_21	1 000	2 150	4587.92	4548.60	4616.50	1.00
TC_P_22	2 000	3 730	9598.96	9405.94	9725.28	2.09
TC_P_23	3 000	4 909	14548.35	14350.38	14714.94	3.17
TC_P_24	4 000	5 648	19791.52	19395.85	20048.88	4.31
TC_P_25	5 000	6 212	24803.27	24603.33	25094.80	5.41
TC_P_26	10 000	7 265	54764.76	54206.57	55252.98	11.94
TC_P_21_b	1 000	2 150	4946.49	4886.69	4984.89	1.00
TC_P_22_b	2 000	3 730	10692.24	10487.35	10795.47	2.16
TC_P_23_b	3 000	4 909	17360.08	17329.65	17379.97	3.51
TC_P_24_b	4 000	5 648	24502.99	24450.30	24543.21	4.95
TC_P_25_b	5 000	6 212	32164.10	31826.07	32601.67	6.50
TC_P_26_b	10 000	7 265	84363.13	84131.88	84591.67	17.06

Suite 1 suggests an almost linear scaling of runtime as a function of
the number of agents (at least for small numbers of agents up to 200).

In contrast, suite 2 illustrates clearly the effect of constraints within
a model (see also Figure 9.14). Whereas the runtime growths almost
linearly for test cases without constraint, the presence of a constraint

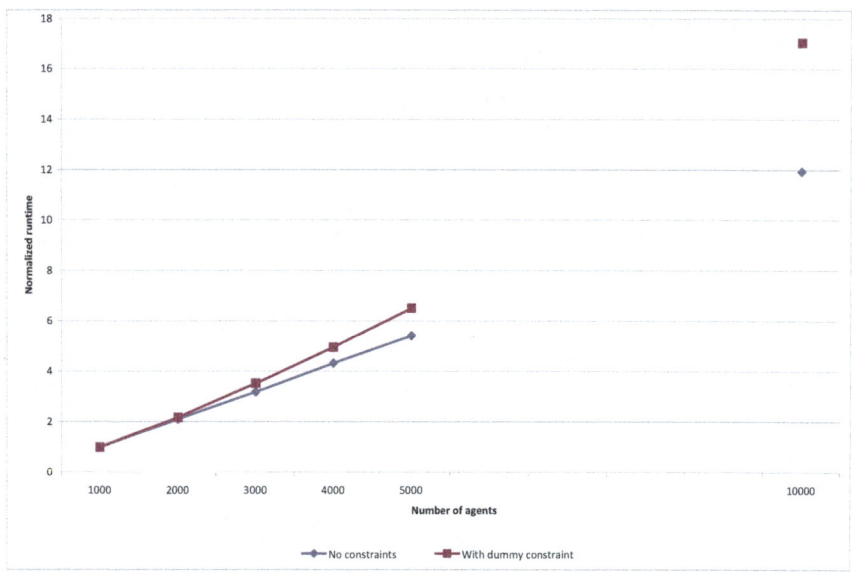

Figure 9.14: Results of benchmark suite 2.

leads to a significantly steeper growth of runtime. This effect is more evident if more agents are present in the model.

In theory, constraints lead to a quadratic growth of runtime (see Section 8.1.2). The benchmarks with up to 10 000 agents indicate that (by regression analysis) the runtime depends on the number of agents in the following way: $t_r = 0.08n_A^2 + 0.91n_A + 0.034$. Of course, these coefficients are highly dependent on the chosen model and the implementation of the specific simulation engine. Furthermore, the coefficients are highly sensitive to, at least, two factors:

- Time for evaluating a constraint
  The most influential impact factor is the time needed for a single evaluation of a constraint. Within the presented benchmark suites, the dummy constraint contains no actual logic, but only a number of loops and string operations in order to consume time. The more complex a constraint is, the more computation and data is necessary to evaluate a constraint. Assuming $O(n_A^2)$ constraint evaluations,

the time required for a single evaluation of a constraint has a huge impact on overall runtime.

• Number of constraints
Besides the time required for evaluating a single constraint, the number of constraints is another major impact factor on overall runtime. The overall runtime growths linearly with the number of constraints to be evaluated.

Within benchmark suite 2, only a single constraint is considered and the time required for a single evaluation of this constraint is fixed. Nevertheless, the impact of the presence of constraints is demonstrated.

9.5.4 Benchmark suite 3: Parallelization on node-level

Benchmark suite 3 is intended to demonstrate potential runtime reduction by using a parallelized simulation engine.

Setup suite 3

All benchmarks in suite 3 operate on the same environment env05:

• Size: 1 500 × 1 500 cells

• 20 000 obstacles (randomly placed walls)

• 40 000 randomly placed tiles

• 1 500 randomly placed holes

This benchmark suite uses a single-threaded event-driven simulation engine and a multi-threaded event-driven simulation engine. Each simulation has a duration of 100 time steps (simulation time). The test cases are documented in Table 9.6. The simulation time and the environment are fixed, the parameter being varied is the number of agents as well as the simulation engine.

Table 9.6: Setup of test cases for benchmark suite 3.

Test case	Nr of agents	Simulation engine	Partitioning strategy
TC_P_31	1 000	single-threaded	–
TC_P_32	2 000	single-threaded	–
TC_P_33	3 000	single-threaded	–
TC_P_34	4 000	single-threaded	–
TC_P_35	5 000	single-threaded	–
TC_P_36	10 000	single-threaded	–
TC_P_31_b	1 000	multi-threaded	node-level/per agent/static
TC_P_32_b	2 000	multi-threaded	node-level/per agent/static
TC_P_33_b	3 000	multi-threaded	node-level/per agent/static
TC_P_34_b	4 000	multi-threaded	node-level/per agent/static
TC_P_35_b	5 000	multi-threaded	node-level/per agent/static
TC_P_36_b	10 000	multi-threaded	node-level/per agent/static

The simulations using a multi-threaded simulation engine are all executed with 4 threads. All test cases are performed with the dummy constraint available.

Results, analysis and interpretation

The results of benchmark suite 3 are shown in Table 9.7. The multi-threaded simulation execution achieves a speedup up to 3.78 which is close to the maximum (considering the 4-core processor used for executing the parallelized (multi-threaded) simulation engine).

Table 9.7: Results of test cases for benchmark suite 3 (3 runs of each test case).

Test case	Runtime in seconds			Normalized runtime	
	Avg	Min	Max		Speedup
TC_P_31	4946.49	4886.69	4984.89	1.00	–
TC_P_32	10692.24	10487.35	10795.47	2.16	–
TC_P_33	17360.08	17329.65	17379.97	3.51	–
TC_P_34	24502.99	24450.30	24543.21	4.95	–
TC_P_35	32164.10	31826.07	32601.67	6.50	–
TC_P_36	84363.13	84131.88	84591.67	17.06	–
TC_P_31_b	1513.95	1460.53	1541.20	1.00	3.27
TC_P_32_b	3196.51	3076.18	3302.80	2.11	3.34
TC_P_33_b	4845.05	4825.59	4859.05	3.20	3.58
TC_P_34_b	6843.09	6792.73	6896.85	4.52	3.58
TC_P_35_b	8975.29	8773.26	9097.52	5.93	3.58
TC_P_36_b	22319.88	22113.02	22466.38	14.74	3.78

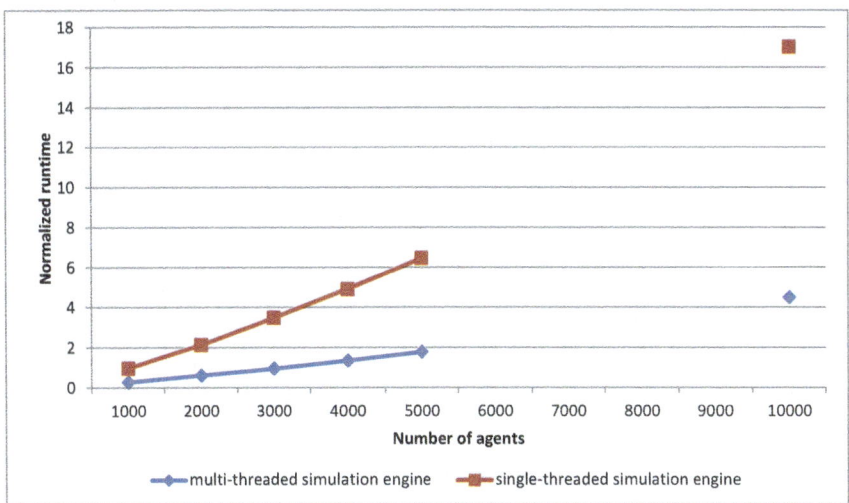

Figure 9.15: Results of benchmark suite 3.

10 Summary

Agent-based models are characterized by an inherent parallelism as all agents act simultaneously. Trying to exploit this parallelism by an adequate simulation engine seems natural. The main problem is that agent-based models are not only characterized by agents acting simultaneously, but also by agents interacting with each other in complex and manifold ways. The interactions between agents effectively limit the degree of possible parallelization and demand appropriate decomposition of a model into independent partitions.

Evaluating constraints defined within an agent-based model and computing the result of concurrent actions takes $O(n^2)$ time (with n referring to the number of agents). This quadratic growth of runtime severely limits scalability and needs to be reduced in order to gain significant speedups. Decomposing the set of agents into sets of agents which may be executed in parallel is an improvement as the quadratic growth now applies to smaller sets of agents.

As the choice of a suitable model partitioning strategy is significant for achieving a high speedup, various partitioning strategies are presented. The partitioning strategies are divided into strategies operating on a *per-agent* basis and on strategies operating on a *per-action* basis. Per agent means that agents are treated as a whole whereas per action refers to strategies which operate on the finer scale of sensor and effector actions of agents. The actual partitioning may be either uninformed or take into account additional information. Typical information to be taken into account is the spatial distribution of agents. The assumption is that agents far away from each other do not influence each other. Other information which may be taken into account for creating a good partitioning are communication and interaction relations between agents.

Defining partitioning strategies is the easy task; the hard part is to actually compute a partitioning. An optimal partitioning strategy ensures that a maximum number of agents may be executed in parallel. Computing the desired number of partitions of independent agents is equivalent to the graph partitioning problem which is known to be NP-complete. Therefore, computing partitions of independent agents has to rely on heuristic methods. Typical heuristic methods include spatial decomposition as well as action-dependent decomposition.

Given a specific partitioning, it is easy to evaluate its quality *a posteriori* by measuring runtime and calculating the speedup achieved by using this partitioning strategy. Yet, it is hardly possible to evaluate the quality of a partitioning strategy *a priori*. Typical indicators used to evaluate the quality of a specific partitioning include the equality of distribution of agents to partitions, minimization of agent interaction across partition boundaries, minimization of network traffic, etc. Unfortunately, these indicators are often hard to compute and of little predictive value regarding achievable speedup.

Model partitioning has to go hand in hand with parallel execution of the simulation engine that actually executes the model. This thesis defines parallelization of a simulation engine on three levels: At first, parallel execution may be applied on processor-level (i. e., usage of multi-core processors); secondly, parallel execution may be applied on node-level by usage of multiple processors within one computing node and thirdly, parallel execution may be applied on cluster-level by the usage of multiple computing nodes. Multi-level parallelization refers to simultaneous application of parallelization on multiple levels, e. g., by combining cluster-level and node-level parallelization.

An example implementation of the GRAMS reference model has been developed to demonstrate its practical applicability. The example implementation resembles the GRAMS reference model very closely. Two different single-threaded simulation engines were implemented (one using a time-stepped execution control, and the other one using an event-driven execution control) as well as a multi-threaded event-driven simulation engine. As expected all simulation engines produce identical results when executing the same model. The conformance of the simulation engines with the GRAMS reference model is verified by a test suite built around the widely known Tileworld-model.

The example implementation was further used for empirical measurements. Multiple benchmark suites were defined and subsequently executed on different simulation engines. The limiting influence of constraint evaluation on overall runtime was shown in benchmark setups with up to 10 000 agents. Besides this, the practical evaluation confirmed the tacit assumption that the choice of an optimal partitioning strategy is not domain independent, but has to take into account the specific domain of the model at hand.

Part IV

Conclusions

11 Conclusions and outlook

The development, analysis and evaluation of complex systems requires more and more the use of modeling and simulation, as it is often impossible to do otherwise. Often microscopic modeling approaches like agent-based modeling and simulation are used for representing such complex systems. Despite widespread use in many application areas, the foundations of agent-based modeling and simulation are much less profound than in other established modeling paradigms. With special emphasis on agent-based modeling and simulation, this thesis aims at two goals. Firstly, improving effectivity and efficiency of model development and secondly, improving effectivity of model execution.

11.1 Summary

Based on extensive analysis of basics and related work in the area of agent-based modeling and simulation, this thesis identifies the need for a reference model for agent-based modeling and simulation. The newly developed *General Reference Model for Agent-based Modeling and Simulation* (GRAMS) defines on a generic level components and structure of agent-based models as well as the simulation of such models. The GRAMS reference model considers the macro-level as well as the micro-level of agent-based models. The macro-level specifies the simulation time, the simulated environment in which all agents are acting and constraints limiting the agents possibilities to act.

On the micro-level, the GRAMS reference model defines structure and behavior of agents. An agent is characterized by a set of attributes, may perceive its environment by a set of sensors and may interact within the environment by means of effectors. Sensors and effectors of an agent are combined to sensor-effector-chains and define the behavior of an agent. Agents can only try to execute a specific sensor or effector action. The actual outcome is determined by taking into account the current model state and all concurrent actions of all agents. As the actions of two or more agents may be in conflict with each other, the result of each action depends on whether this action is in conflict with any other action. Constraints define exactly under which circumstances the execution of an action is not successful.

In order to provide a solid foundation, the GRAMS reference model separates strictly between an agent-based model itself and its simulation which is executed by appropriate simulation engines. The ability to execute an agent-based model using different simulation engines, each producing identical results, is a central aspect of the GRAMS reference model.

The possibility of using different simulation engines executing the same model is also crucial for exploiting hardware-given parallelism. In this thesis, parallelization of simulation engines is defined on three levels – namely cluster-, node-, and processor-level – with multi-level parallelization referring to the simultaneous application of parallelization on multiple levels. Depending on the underlying hardware, a simulation engine may execute a given model and exploit multi-core processors as well as make use of multiple computing nodes.

The applicability of the GRAMS reference model is demonstrated in two ways. At first, by providing an example implementation of the GRAMS reference model including different simulation engines. Secondly, by evaluating the GRAMS reference model with regard to practical applicability using three case studies.

11.2 Scientific contributions and applicability

This thesis provides two main contributions to current research in the area of agent-based modeling and simulation:

1. The GRAMS reference model provides solid and clear definitions of key aspects of agent-based modeling and simulation. It provides

a valuable basis for getting to a common understanding of agent-based modeling and simulation and has proven its value in several case studies. The GRAMS reference model serves as a framework for effective and efficient development of conceptual and semi-formal agent-based models.

2. The second main contribution is the demonstration of the flexibility and possibilities coming with a strict separation of an agent-based model and its simulation. Conceptually separating a model and its simulation gives rise to the possibility of implementing different simulation engines and using specialized parallelization techniques. This in turn is the necessary prerequisite to enabling the transition from small-scale model development to large-scale models.

The two original goals of this thesis are directly addressed by the developed approach and, although the underlying problems are most probably not finally solved, both goals are achieved:

1. Improving effectivity and efficiency of model development.
The GRAMS reference model provides a solid and coherent foundation of agent-based modeling and simulation. It focuses primarily on the conceptual model development, although it may also guide the development of formal models. Achieving a common understanding of agent-based modeling and simulation within the large community working in this area is a difficult and long process, in which the GRAMS reference model may be considered a first step.

Common understanding of a domain is an absolutely necessary prerequisite for collaborative work. In this sense, the GRAMS reference model helps to enable collaborative development of agent-based models. By strictly separating the definition of a model and its simulation, not only the model itself may be developed in a collaborative manner, but development of models and simulation engines may be separated.

Furthermore, the GRAMS reference model implies a certain sequence of activities during model development and thus guides model developers through a model development process.

2. Improving effectivity of model execution.

The possibility to separate model development from the development of specific simulation engines is very beneficial for bridging the efficiency and programmability gap. Software engineers may focus on the development of simulation engines optimized for the computing hardware at hand while model developers can focus purely on model development.

Regarding the applicability of the solution approach presented in this thesis, two main aspects have to be distinguished:

- The GRAMS reference model may be directly used by anyone working in the area of agent-based modeling and simulation. At the current stage the GRAMS reference model should primarily be used as a guideline for development of conceptual models. Of course, it may also be used to structure development of formal and executable models.

- Regarding parallelization of the simulation of an agent-based model, the limiting factor of constraint evaluation is negligble for small to medium-sized models (up to 10 000 agents). Therefore, the need to parallelize the execution is often not given. Considering large-scale models the presented parallelization approaches may be applied to reduce runtime or to overcome memory limitations.

Instead of executing a single model in parallel, a more appropriate approach in many cases is to execute multiple independent simulations in parallel. If repeated simulations are required due to reasons of statistical analysis, this is a very feasible way to exploit hardware-given parallelism. Yet, enabling parallel execution of a single simulation seems valuable in at least two situations (cp. [56]): Firstly, if it is impossible to simulate a large-scale model on a single computing node due to memory demand of the model. Secondly, if it is crucial to reduce the time until first results are available (e. g., for decision support).

11.3 Outlook

Two areas seem most important for future work: Firstly, tight integration of the GRAMS reference model into model development processes and secondly, providing better suited approaches for parallel execution.

In its current form, the GRAMS reference model targets at supporting the development of conceptual and formal models. Yet, the GRAMS reference model is not tightly integrated into the model development process in a way that easy and fast application would be possible. It would definitely be of great value to provide support on how to use GRAMS reference model to realize its full potential and to ensure high efficiency in its application.

The most challenging aspect when considering parallel execution is the decomposition of an agent-based model into the required number of independent partitions. This thesis did not define completely new partitioning strategies, but organized existing partitioning strategies within a common frame. Therefore, the question remains open whether it is possible to define generic partitioning strategies applicable to agent-based models of various domains. Also, an evaluation which type of partitioning strategy is typically best-suited for a specific classes of agent-based models would be of great interest. Besides these two work areas, reliability and performability issues are also important to look at.

Part V

Appendix

A Case studies of the GRAMS reference model

This chapter presents two case studies of the GRAMS reference model which have been performed to evaluate its practical applicability. Both case studies have partially been published [121], [40, 41, 42].

A.1 Case study: Warehouse

This case study is used as first attempt to evaluate whether the specifications and definitions of the GRAMS reference model are detailed enough and if the GRAMS reference model is practically applicable. The case study deals with the analysis of a typical warehouse scenario and follows closely the model development process as described in Section 2.1.3. In the following sections, the structured problem description and the conceptual model are presented in detail.

This case study has been published in a shortened version [121].

A.1.1 Structured problem description

Problem description

Objectives The objective is to analyze the performance of a simplified warehouse. The case study considers a generic warehouse, workers and forklifts to transport articles and a warehouse manager who is responsible for handling orders as well as managing incoming and outgoing articles.

Especially, the following three more specific objectives are of interest:

1. **Processing time:** The processing time (minimum, average, maximum) for fulfilling an order is the first of two key performance measures for warehouse efficiency. The processing time spans the time period from receiving an order until all required articles are loaded onto an outgoing truck. Two different situations need to be distinguished: The first situation is that all articles are available in the warehouse, whereas in the second situation some (or all) articles have to be reordered by the warehouse manager.

2. **Costs:** Obviously, processing time can always be minimized by using a larger warehouse and more workers respectively forklifts. Therefore, the second key performance measure are the costs. On the one hand, overall costs (i. e., warehouse, workers, forklifts, etc.) are of interest and on the other hand utilization of the warehouse as well as of workers and forklifts.

3. **Usability of the reference model:** This objective aims to answer the question if the GRAMS reference model is able to represent all aspects with the necessary level of detail and if the specifications and definitions of the reference model regarding the simulation of such a model are detailed enough. Due to the fact that no performance measures exist, this objective can not be answered in a quantitative way but only in a qualitative way.

Input parameters   The following input parameters are relevant for the analysis:

- Warehouse setup
  The warehouse setup is defined by several variables. For simplicity, it can be assumed that the warehouse has a rectangular layout. The main area of the warehouse is divided into two disjoint sets:

  – The *storage area* is the area for storage of articles.

  – The *transportation area* is the area for transporting articles from one place to another (either by workers or forklifts). Under no circumstances may articles be stored at the transportation area.

Additionally, *platforms* are used for loading and unloading trucks. Each platform serves as an intermediate storage area and has capacity for the equivalent of one truck. Furthermore, each platform is used exclusively for incoming or outgoing trucks. Therefore, the actual setup of a warehouse consists of the following parts:

– Overall size of the main area (rectangular layout).

– Size and placement of storage and transportation areas.

– Number and placement of platforms for incoming and outgoing trucks.

It is assumed that platforms are not part of the warehouse itself, but are adjacent to its main area.

- Initial inventory
  The initial inventory describes exactly which articles (name, quantity, storage location) are in stock at the beginning of the simulation.

- Workers
  Workers are required to transport articles from one place to another. It has to be specified how many workers are available and where they are situated at the beginning of the simulation. Furthermore, individual costs have to be defined for each worker.

- Forklifts
  Forklifts can be treated similarly to workers. They are able to transport larger articles and have different individual costs.

- List of orders
  The orders which the warehouse manager has to fulfill are given in a deterministic way, i. e., the list of orders contains all orders which have to be fulfilled during a simulation. The list of orders defines exactly at which point in time a specific order will be received by the warehouse manager.

Output parameters According to the objectives, the output parameters listed in Table A.1 have been chosen.

Table A.1: Output parameters.

Name	Unit	Description
Processing time	minutes	The processing time (minimum, average, maximum) spans the time period from receiving an order until all required articles are loaded onto an outgoing truck. Two different situations are distinguished: The first situation is that all articles are available in the warehouse, whereas in the second situation some (or all) articles have to be reordered by the warehouse manager.
Costs	Euro	The costs are determined by the size of the warehouse (fixed costs), the value of the inventory and the number of workers and forklifts.
Utilization	%	The utilization (minimum, average, maximum) of the warehouse is defined as the ratio of occupied storage area to the overall storage area. Similarly, the utilization of workers and forklifts is defined as the ratio of the time period they are actually working (i. e., transporting articles) to the overall simulated time.

Description of real system

Objects, structure, properties and interactions   The following objects of the real system have to be modeled (including their main characteristics):

- Article types
  - Article name
  - Value (in Euro)
  - Weight
  - Reordering time: The reordering time denotes the time of delivery which is required for reordering articles.

- Articles
  - Unique article identifier (e. g., CM1234)
  - Reference to article type
  - Status: available, reserved/not available

  It is assumed that all articles (regardless of article type) require the same amount of storage area.

- Orders
  - Unique order identifier (e. g., OR1889)
  - Order date
  - Order items (i. e., article type and quantity)

- Warehouse (as described above)

  The *warehouse manager* is responsible for all activities within the whole warehouse:

- Receiving incoming orders.

- Commanding workers and forklifts.

- Deciding about storage plan.

- Reordering missing articles.

The workers and forklifts are (more or less) identical:

- Maximum payload (in kg).

- Speed (in m/s).

- Required time for picking up respectively putting down an article (in seconds).

- Possible states: available, in use, out of order.

Use case 1: Incoming order, everything available   This use case is characterized by the fact that all resources necessary for executing an incoming order are available:

- All articles required for fulfilling an incoming order are available at the warehouse.

- All required workers and forklifts are available.

- An outgoing platform is available.

From the warehouse managers point of view, the workflow is the following:

1. Warehouse manager receives an order.

2. As all ordered articles are available, the status of all ordered articles is changed from *available* to *reserved.*

3. An available outgoing platform is selected and the status of this platform is changed from *unassigned* to *assigned.*

4. Depending on the ordered articles the warehouse manager commands workers and forklifts to transport the articles from their storage locations to the selected outgoing platform.

5. The workers and forklifts transport the articles to the platform.

6. As soon as all articles are transported to the platform, the order is fulfilled and the status of the platform is changed to *unassigned.*

From the workers point of view, the workflow looks like this:

1. The worker receives a command which includes the point of origin and destination of an article. New status: *in use*

2. The worker moves towards the point of origin and picks up the article.

3. The worker transports the article to the destination and puts it down. New status: *available*

Obviously, if an order consists of multiple articles the workflow for a worker or forklift is executed multiple times.

Use case 2: Incoming order, some articles have to be reordered
Contrary to the use case 1, this use case is characterized by the fact that not all required articles are available at the warehouse. From the warehouse managers point of view, the workflow is the following:

1. Warehouse manager receives an order.

2. For all articles which are already available in the warehouse the status is changed to *reserved.*

3. An available outgoing platform is selected and the status of this platform is changed to *assigned.*

4. All missing articles are reordered.

5. As soon as the missing articles are delivered, they are transported directly to the outgoing platform.

6. Depending on the ordered articles the warehouse manager commands workers and forklifts to transport the articles from the storage locations to the outgoing platform.

7. The workers and forklifts transport the articles to the platform.

8. As soon as all articles are transported to the outgoing platform, the order is fulfilled and the status of the platform is changed to *unassigned*.

Use case 3: Incoming articles Due to scheduled deliveries and reorders of the warehouse manager, articles are regularly delivered to the warehouse. In this case, the workflow of the warehouse manager is the following:

- A delivery truck arrives at an available incoming platform.

- As long as storage locations are available, the warehouse manager commands workers and forklifts to transport the articles from the incoming platform to the storage locations.

- As soon as all articles are transported to their storage locations, the platform is available again for the next truck.

Model requirements

Structural elements

- Warehouse: The warehouse setup is static, i. e., it does not change within a simulation.

- Workers and forklifts: The number of workers and forklifts is constant.

- Trucks: The incoming and outgoing trucks are not part of the model.

- Warehouse manager: The warehouse manager is a key element. He is responsible for all activities in the warehouse, commands workers and forklifts, organizes storage allocation and processes incoming orders.

Constraints

- All articles have the same size.

- Each reorder is executed independently of other reorders, especially no reorders are combined.

- Each order and reorder fits in a single truck.

A.1.2 Conceptual model

Model overview

Target parameters The following target parameters are defined:

- Processing time: The processing time spans the time period from receiving an order until all required articles are loaded onto an outgoing truck. Two different situations are distinguished: The first situation is that all articles are available in the warehouse, whereas in the second situation some (or all) articles have to be reordered by the warehouse manager.

Name	Unit	Description
PT_{min}	minutes	Minimum Processing Time, all articles available.
PT_{avg}	minutes	Average Processing Time, all articles available.
PT_{max}	minutes	Maximum Processing Time, all articles available.
PT^r_{min}	minutes	Minimum Processing Time, articles have to be reordered.
PT^r_{avg}	minutes	Average Processing Time, articles have to be reordered.
PT^r_{max}	minutes	Maximum Processing Time, articles have to be reordered.

- Costs: The costs are determined by the size of the warehouse, the average inventory and the number of workers and forklifts.

Name	Unit	Description
C_{all}	Euro	Overall costs (warehouse, workers, forklifts), without taking inventory into account.
C_{inv}	Euro	Average value of inventory (Precision: minutes)
U^S_{min}	%	Minimum utilization of warehouse.
U^S_{avg}	%	Average utilization of warehouse.
U^S_{max}	%	Maximum utilization of warehouse.
U^W_{min}	%	Minimum utilization of workers.
U^W_{avg}	%	Average utilization of workers.
U^W_{max}	%	Maximum utilization of workers.
U^F_{min}	%	Minimum utilization of forklifts.
U^F_{avg}	%	Average utilization of forklifts.
U^F_{max}	%	Maximum utilization of forklifts.

Irrelevant objects and aspects of real system

- Incoming and outgoing trucks are not part of the model. Instead, the platforms for incoming and outgoing articles form the model boundary.

- The size of articles is neglected, i. e., all articles have the same size.

Decomposition into submodels   As illustrated in Figure A.1 the model is decomposed into the submodels SM 1, SM 2, and SM 3 which represent the components of the GRAMS reference model.

Macro-level: Simulation time

For the *simulation time*, a discrete time domain is chosen, i. e., $\mathbb{T} = \mathbb{N} = \{0, 1, 2, \dots\}$. It is assumed that the simulation starts at an arbitrary point in time $t_{\text{start}} = 0$ and ends at t_{end}. In order to allow a precise description of the movement of workers and forklifts a single time step represents 0.1 seconds. Table A.2 illustrates the relation of simulation time to real time.

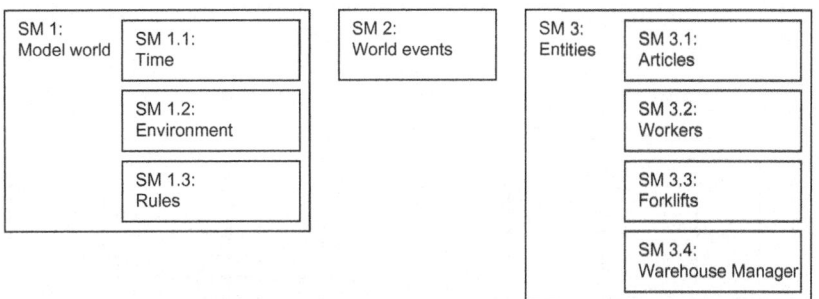

Figure A.1: Decomposition of the model into submodels SM 1, SM 2, and SM 3.

Table A.2: Relation of simulation time to real time.

Simulation time $\mathbb{T}$	0	1	2	3	4	5	6	...
Real time [s]	0	0.1	0.2	0.3	0.4	0.5	0.6	...

Macro-level: Environment

The floor-layout of the warehouse is modeled as a rectangular, grid-like environment. A schematic of the environment is shown in Figure A.2. Each cell of the grid has a size of $1\,\text{m} \times 1\,\text{m}$ and can be uniquely identified by its (x, y)-coordinates, with the origin $(0, 0)$ being in the upper-left corner:

$$\mathbb{L} = \{ \quad (0,0), \quad (1,0), \quad \dots, \quad (n_x - 1, 0),$$
$$(0,1), \quad (1,1), \quad \dots, \quad (n_x - 1, 1),$$
$$\vdots \qquad \vdots \qquad \ddots \qquad \vdots \tag{A.1}$$
$$(0, n_y - 1), \quad (1, n_y - 1), \quad \dots, \quad (n_x - 1, n_y - 1) \quad \}$$

The cells are distinguished into two different types:

- Storage area
  The storage area allows storage of articles. It is asssumed that articles are not stacked on top of each other. Furthermore, the

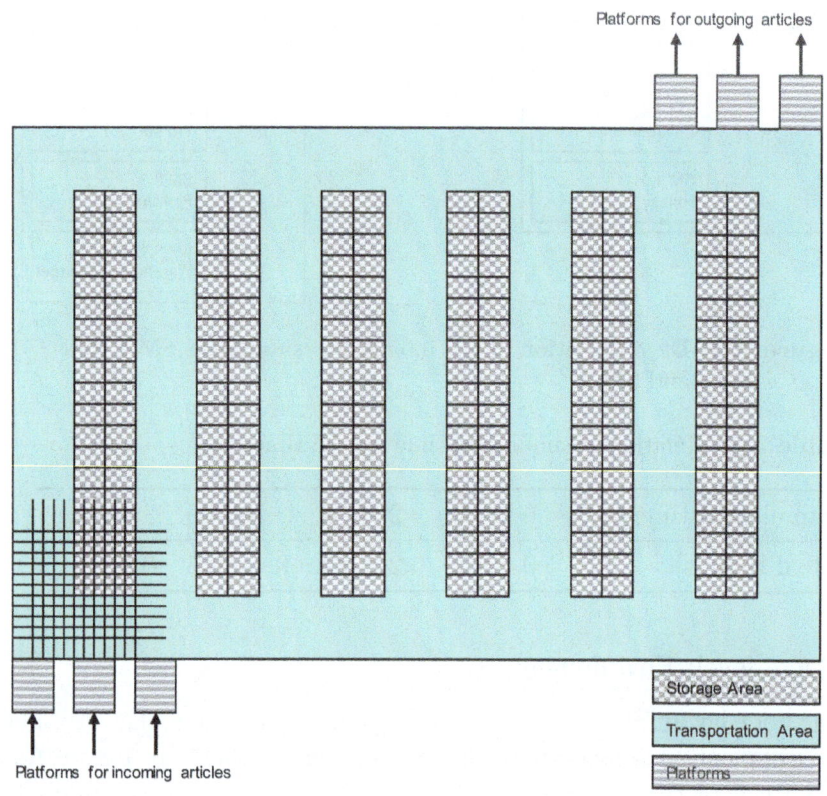

Figure A.2: Schematics of the warehouse environment.

storage area may not be walked or driven upon. At the moment, the storage area is not subdivided any further into storage locations. Therefore, each article may be stored on any cell which is denoted as storage area and is currently not occupied by another article.

- Transportation area
  The transportation area defines the driveways which may be used by workers or forklifts to carry articles from one place to another. The transportation area is assumed to be always clear of articles and other obstacles.

A property p_{type} denotes the cell type:

$$\mathbb{P} = \{ \quad p_{\text{type}} : \mathbb{L} \rightarrow \{storage, transportation\}\} \qquad \text{(A.2)}$$

Boundary cells may be connected to a platform. Platforms represent areas for incoming respectively outgoing articles. It is assumed that articles can be taken from a platform for incoming articles as long as articles are available and that a worker respectively forklift has to be on an adjacent cell while picking-up an article. The same reasoning applies to outgoing articles, i.e., as long as a worker or forklift is on an adjacent cell and a platform for outgoing articles provides enough free space, articles may be put onto it. For simplicity, it is assumed that incoming as well as outgoing platforms are not limited in the number of articles that may be put onto the platform (i.e., no upper limit).

No update functions are defined: $\mathbb{U} = \emptyset$.

Macro-level: Constraints

Constraints define conditions under which a single action of an agent may be executed successfully or fails. Actions may fail due to environmental circumstances which are not under the control of an agent. Constraints are used to define in which case actions of two (or more) agents are in conflict with each other. By default, all actions of the agents are executed successfully and no two actions of any agents influence each other. For this model, the set of constraints $\mathbb{C} = \{c_1, c_2\}$ is quite simple:

- $c_1 \in \mathbb{C}$: Only one worker or forklift may be at a specific cell at the same time.
  If two workers or forklifts try to move to the same cell at the same time, a collision occurs. Due to this collision, both parties are *out of order* for 5 minutes. The collision is represented by a specific event type, namely *Collision*-events. Each time a violation of this constraint is detected (i.e., more than two agents being on the same cell or two or more agents moving onto the same cell), a

Collision-event is triggered which in turn leads to an unsuccessful completion of the agents' actions (i. e., their movement onto this cell).

- $c_2 \in \mathbb{C}$: Worker or forklift has to be on adjacent cell for picking-up and putting-down articles.
  In order to pick-up an article or put-down an article, workers and forklifts have to be on a cell adjacent to a storage location respectively an incoming or outgoing platform. By explicitly stating and modeling this condition as a constraint in the sense of the GRAMS reference model, appropriate simulation engines are capable of enforcing this constraint during a simulation execution. Thereby, flaws in behavior or subtle implementation errors are detected fast. Compared to constraint c_1 a violation of this constraint does not result in a new event, but leads to an abortion of the current simulation, i. e., if a simulation engine detects a violation of constraint c_2 the current simulation is stopped immediately.

Micro-level: Articles

A clear distinction has to be made between *articles* and *article types*. An article type contains general information and does not refer to a real, physical article. Therefore, article types are characterized by the following properties:

- Unique name (e. g., coffee machine)

- Weight
  Only two different weights are distinguished: light, heavy. *Light articles* may be carried by either persons or forklifts. *Heavy articles* may only be carried by forklifts.

- Value (in Euro)

- Reordering time
  The reordering time denotes the time of delivery which is required in case of reorders of the warehouse manager. Unit: minutes.

Articles represent physical objects which are stored in the warehouse. Each article is fully characterized by the following attributes:

- $b_1 \in \mathbb{ATT}$: Unique article identifier

- $b_2 \in \mathbb{ATT}$: Article type

- $b_3 \in \mathbb{ATT}$: Status
  The status may be either *available* indicating that this article is still available (e. g., for incoming orders) or *reserved* in which case the article is already assigned to an order and no longer available.

It is assumed that each article requires a single cell for storage, i. e., no article spans more than one cell and one cell cannot be used for storage of more than one article.

Micro-level: Worker

A worker may walk around in the warehouse and transport light articles. A worker is assumed to occupy one cell no matter if he carries an article or not. Furthermore, each worker is equipped with the following knowledge:

- Warehouse setup, i. e., each worker knows the exact placement of storage areas, transportation areas and platforms.

- As the workers may receive commands from the warehouse manager (like 'Transport article a_1 from storage area $(15, 20)$ to platform out_1.'), each worker is able to store the last command given to him in his internal knowledge base.

The behavior of a worker-agent is determined by its sensors and effectors. Each worker-agent is equipped with the following two sensors:

- A *Perceive*-sensor allows a worker-agent to perceive its environment and therefore reflects some kind of optical perception. For simplicity (and as the required adaptations would just be rather technical), a bounded perception (e. g., only neighboring cells within a limited distance) is not necessary. A single perceive-action takes 0.5 seconds, or equivalently 5 time steps within the defined simulation time.

- A *Receive*-sensor is used to receive incoming communication messages. The only incoming communication are the commands which the warehouse manager may send to a worker-agent. An action of this sensor includes the reception of the message itself as well as storing the received message in the internal knowledge base, and is therefore assumed to take 3 seconds (30 steps within the simulation time).

Besides these sensor actions, each worker-agent is capable of the following four effector actions:

- A *Move*-effector allows a worker-agent to move to a neighboring cell (diagonal moves are allowed). Each action of this effector represents exactly one movement and takes 1 second (10 time steps).

- Picking up articles (either from a platform or storage area) is modeled by a *Pick-Up*-effector and takes 5 seconds (50 time steps). Additional conditions, like maximum transportation capabilities of worker-agents, may be defined and enforced via appropriate constraints, but are omitted within this case study.

- In the same way as picking up articles, putting down articles is modeled by a *Put-Down*-effector and takes also 5 seconds.

- While the previous three effectors directly alter the environment (or at least, try to do so), the fourth effector is of a different kind. The *Plan*-effector is an endogenous effector representing the internal planning process of a worker-agent. As planning is assumed to be an ongoing process, a single plan-action takes only 1 time step.

The sensors and effectors determine the general capabilities of a worker-agent; the actual behavior is defined by the interplay of the sensors and effectors. Figure A.3 illustrates the interplay in the form

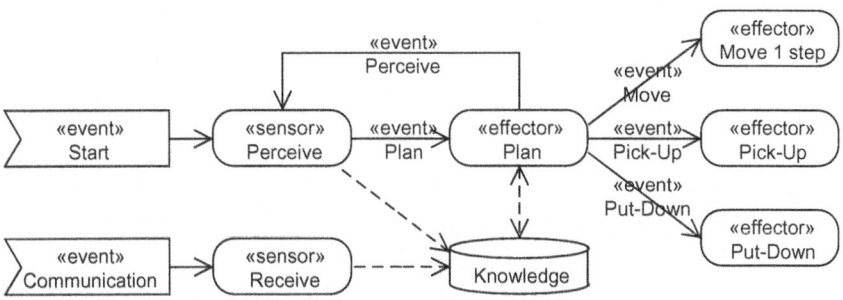

Figure A.3: Sensor-effector-chains of a worker-agent.

of *Sensor-Effector-chains*. As can be seen, the sensor-effector-chains combine the sensor and effector actions into a meaningful sequence. Initially, each worker-agent receives a *Start*-event at the beginning of a simulation. This event triggers the main loop of a worker-agent consisting of the Perceive-sensor and the Plan-effector. This main loop is executed by a worker-agent until the end of a simulation no matter what happens. The Receive-sensor on the other hand is only triggered by a Communication-event and stores incoming communication messages into the agents' knowledge base.

The autonomous behavior of a worker-agent is defined completely within the Plan-Action and quite simple: As long as no command is given by the warehouse manager, worker-agents stay at their current location and do nothing. As soon as the Receive-sensor of a worker-agent is triggered, the worker-agent receives and stores the incoming communication message into its internal knowledge base. Currently, the possible set of communication messages is restricted to Transport-Commands. Each Transport-Command consists of a point of origin and a destination. First, a worker-agent has to move towards the point of origin. Once it arrives it picks up the article which is located there and transports it to the destination where it puts the article down.

Figure A.4 shows the state chart of a worker-agent: As long as a worker-agent has not received any command, it is in *Idle*-state. After

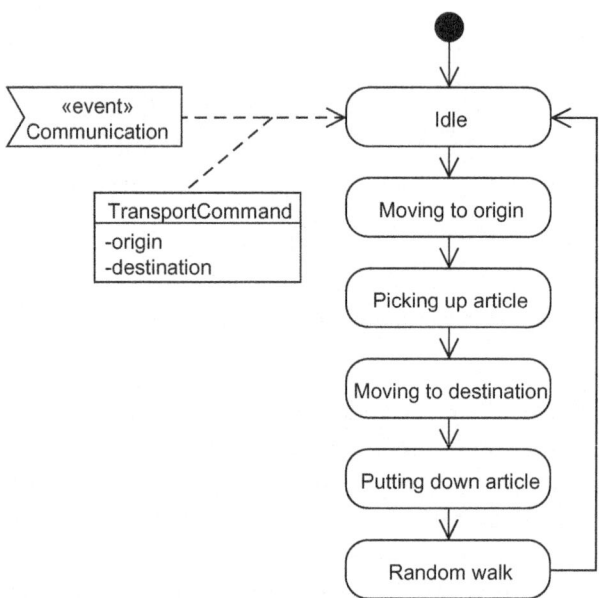

Figure A.4: State chart of a worker-agent.

receiving a Transport-Command, this new information is taken into account by the repeatedly executed Plan-effector and the worker-agent starts moving directly to the specified origin. Upon arrival at the origin, it picks up the article (either from an incoming platform or a storage location), and moves to the designated destination. At the destination, the worker-agent puts the transported article down (either to a storage location or to an outgoing platform). Afterwards, the worker-agent moves to a randomly chosen location within the warehouse and waits for new commands.

Micro-level: Forklifts

Essentially, forklifts are modeled in the same way as workers i. e., they are capable of the same actions and exhibit the same behavior. The only difference is the transport capacity: While worker-agents may only carry light articles, forklift-agents may also carry heavy articles.

Micro-level: Warehouse manager

The third agent type, the warehouse manager, is responsible for distributing tasks to workers and forklifts. It has knowledge about all articles (incoming, outgoing, stored) and all agents (persons and forklifts) as well as of currently open orders which need to be fulfilled. Based on these information, the warehouse manager creates appropriate Transport-Commands and sends them to workers and forklifts. The warehouse manager agent has the following knowledge:

- Inventory = storage location × (article | *free*) × (*available* | *reserved*)
  The inventory contains all information about articles currently stored in the warehouse. Free storage locations are available, i. e., articles may be put onto them, as long as they are not reserved for any articles. After ordering a worker or forklift to bring an article to a storage location, this storage location is reserved and is no longer available.

- List of current orders = platform → order
  The list of current orders contains all orders which are processed at this moment. To process an order, a platform has to be available. Once an order has been assigned to a platform, this platform is *busy* until the order is completely fulfilled.

- List of open orders = order*
  The list of open orders contains all orders which have to be processed in future. By default, the warehouse manager agent follows a simple FIFO-strategy, i. e., orders are processed in order of their arrival.

- List of fulfilled orders = order*
  The list of fulfilled orders contains all orders which have been fulfilled until the current point in time.

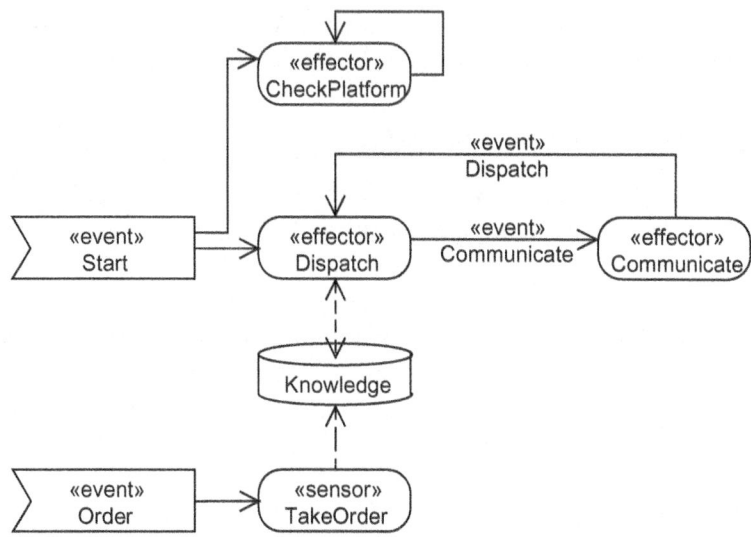

Figure A.5: Sensor-effector-chains of the warehouse manager agent.

- Worker allocation table = worker → (command | *available*)
  The worker allocation table contains information about all workers,
  i. e., if they are currently executing a command or not.

- Forklift allocation table = forklift → (command | *available*)
  Same as worker allocation table.

Figure A.5 illustrates the behavior of the warehouse manager agent.
As depicted, it is equipped with three effectors and one sensor:

- Once the warehouse manager agent has received a Start-event,
  the *Dispatch*-effector takes into account the internal knowledge
  (especially open orders) and is responsible for the whole planning
  process. As dispatching is a time-consuming process, each action of
  this effector takes 30 seconds (300 time steps).

- The *Communicate*-effector communicates devised plans to the respective agents. Each activation takes 5 seconds (50 time steps).

Afterwards, the Dispatch-effector is triggered again. This loop of dispatching and communicating defines the basic behavior of the warehouse manager agent and is executed throughout a simulation.

- Besides triggering the main loop described above, the Start-event also triggers a *CheckPlatform*-effector. To be aware of the status of the plaforms (incoming and outgoing), the warehouse manager agent cyclically checks all platforms. Each action of this effector refers to the check of exactly one platform. Checking a single platform takes 10 seconds (100 time steps).

- The *TakeOrder*-sensor of the warehouse manager agent is activated by an Order-event and updates the internal knowledge (i. e., adds a new order to the list of open orders). This sensor action takes 10 seconds (100 time steps).

Events

The following exogenous events may occur in the simulation:

- *Start*-Event
  Special event denoting the start of the simulation. This event is sent to all agents at the beginning of a simulation.

- Communication-Event
  This event is triggered each time some communication is exchanged between agents. As illustrated in Figure A.4, each communication event transports a TransportCommand to the receiving agent.

- Collision-Event
  If two agents are moving to the same cell in the same moment a collision occurs which is indicated by this event. Both agents remain at their *old* cell, all sensor- and effector-activities are terminated immediately and both agents are *out-of-order* for 15 minutes (9 000 time steps). After these 15 minutes both agents receive a Start-event and resume their regular behavior.

- Order-Event
  The Order-event is sent to the warehouse manager agent and denotes the receipt of a new order.

Additionally, endogenous events within single agents may occur.

A.2 Case study: Joint Fire Support

Joint Fire Support (JFS) is a military term for providing lethal engagements in an ad-hoc manner in highly dynamic warfighting scenarios. JFS requests are typically launched in tactical situations by military ground units confronted with non-predictable threats which can not be engaged by organic engagement means of these ground units. JFS is realized by military engagement, reconnaissance and on scene coordination means provided by army, air force and navy units. These functional nodes are assigned and combined ad-hoc.

A typical JFS request shall be executed within few minutes including the following tasks: determine adequate reconnaissance and engagement assets, check rules of engagement, task and reposition assets, collect and provide adequate target data, conduct and assess the (lethal) engagement. A lot of military command nodes on different command levels may be involved in processing JFS requests properly and in accordance with the given rules of engagement. As JFS requests can not be exactly forecasted in time, target location or class nearly everything has to be coordinated ad-hoc.

A variety of national coordination patterns has evolved in western countries including israeli armed forces to handle this JFS problem domain. A coordination pattern describes the command and control communication structure of command-, engagement- and reconnaissance-nodes in order to collectively provide JFS services. None of the existing coordination patterns seems to be adequate in every situation. Each one has advantages as well as disadvantages. An optimal JFS coordination pattern has to consider the extent and landscape of the operational area of own forces, the amount of expected JFS requests, defined areas of responsibilities of command nodes, the amount of engagement, reconnaissance and on scene coordination means capable to process JFS tasks as well as the applicable chain of command and the political rules of engagement. JFS services may be performed by international forces (a so-called joint/combined setting) introducing additional decision making processes and aspects.

In order to compare different coordination patterns in joint fire support (JFS) scenarios, an agent-based model was developed [40, 41, 42]. This model was developed for analyzing the question at hand and for evaluating the GRAMS reference model.

By following the GRAMS reference model to develop the JFS model, the model developers could focus purely on domain-specific issues. In this sense, the GRAMS reference model served well as a guideline throughout the model development process.

The strict seperation of events and actions defined by the GRAMS reference model turned out to be helpful also. This separation allowed the definition of complex event-action chains where each event could trigger different actions at the same time, whereas these actions could produce events as well. While being beneficial, these event-action chains caused trouble at the same time. In fact, it turned out that they could hardly be analyzed and debugged. This is not necessarily a drawback of the GRAMS reference model, but has at least two reasons: First, the tool chain currently available does not support all aspects of the GRAMS reference model very well and debugging features are far from complete. Second, and perhaps more notably, this complexity of modeling coordination patterns may be immanent to these kind of models.

Bibliography

[1] 50 facts about Agent-Based Computing. AgentLink, 2005.

[2] Die Programmierbarkeit von Multicores fordert uns heraus. Computer Zeitung, Nr. 18, 27 April 2009, April 2009. Konradin Verlag, Leinfelden-Echterdingen.

[3] International Technology Roadmap for Semiconductors 2009 Edition – Design. http://www.itrs.net/Links/2009ITRS/ 2009Chapters_2009Tables/2009_Design.pdf, 2009.

[4] Repast. http://repast.sourceforge.net, 2011.

[5] JADE – Java Agent DEvelopment Framework. http://jade. tilab.com/, June 2012.

[6] Brandon G. Aaby, Kalyan S. Perumalla, and Sudip K. Seal. Efficient Simulation of Agent-Based Models on Multi-GPU and Multi-Core Clusters. In *SIMUTools '10: Proceedings of the 3rd International ICST Conference on Simulation Tools and Techniques*, pages 1–10, ICST, Brussels, Belgium, 2010. ICST (Institute for Computer Sciences, Social-Informatics and Telecommunications Engineering).

[7] Susanne Albers. Onlinealgorithmen. *Informatik Spektrum*, 33(5):438–443, October 2010.

[8] Robert Axelrod. Advancing the Art of Simulation in the Social Sciences. *Journal of the Japan Society for Management Information*, 12(3):3–16, December 2003. Special Issue on *Agent-based Approach: Toward a New Paradigm of Management Informatics*, http://ci.nii.ac.jp/naid/110002914439/en/.

[9] Robert Axelrod. Simulation in the Social Sciences. In Jean-Philippe Rennard, editor, *Handbook of Research on Nature-inspired Computing for Economics and Management*, pages 90–100, Hershey, PA, USA, 2007. Idea Group Inc.

[10] Robert Axtell. Why Agents? On the Varied Motivations for Agent Computing in the Social Sciences. In Charles M. Macal and David Sallach, editors, *Proceedings of the Workshop on Agent Simulation: Applications, Models, and Tools*, pages 3–24, 2000. October 15-16, 1999 The University of Chicago.

[11] Jang Won Bae, GeunHo Lee, and Il-Chull Moon. Formal specification supporting incremental and flexible agent-based modeling. In Laroque et al. [73].

[12] Osman Balci and William F. Ormsby. Conceptual modelling for designing large-scale simulations. *Journal of Simulation*, 1(3):175–186, August 2007.

[13] Stefania Bandini, Sara Manzoni, and Giuseppe Vizzari. Agent Based Modeling and Simulation: An Informatics Perspective. *Journal of Artificial Societies and Social Simulation*, 12(4), October 2009. http://jasss.soc.surrey.ac.uk/12/4/4.html.

[14] Stefania Bandini and Giuseppe Vizzari. Regulation Function of the Environment in Agent-Based Simulation. In Danny Weyns, H. Van Dyke Parunak, and Fabien Michel, editors, *Environments for Multi-Agent Systems III*, volume 4389 of *Lecture Notes in Computer Science*, pages 157–169, Berlin, Heidelberg, 2007. Springer-Verlag. Third International Workshop, E4MAS 2006, Hakodate, Japan, May 8, 2006, Selected Revised and Invited Papers.

[15] Steven C. Bankes. Agent-based modeling: A revolution? *Proceedings of the National Academy of Sciences of the United States of America*, 99(Suppl. 3):7199–7200, May 2002. doi:10.1073/pnas.072081299.

[16] Jerry Banks, John S. Carson II, Barry L. Nelson, and David M. Nicol. *Discrete-Event System Simulation*. Prentice-Hall, 4 edition, 2005.

[17] Fernando J. Barros. Modeling Formalisms for Dynamic Structure Systems. *ACM Transactions on Modeling and Computer Simulation*, 7(4):501–515, October 1997. http://doi.acm.org/10.1145/268403.268423.

[18] Ana L. C. Bazzan and Franziska Klügl, editors. *Multi-Agent Systems for Traffic and Transportation*. IGI Global, 2009.

[19] Kurt Binder and Dieter W. Heermann. *Monte Carlo Simulation in Statistical Physics*, volume 80 of *Springer Series in Solid-State Sciences*. Springer-Verlag, Berlin, Heidelberg, New York, 1 edition, 1988.

[20] Diane P. Bischak and Stephen D. Roberts. Object-Oriented Simulation. In Barry L. Nelson, W. David Kelton, and Gordon M. Clark, editors, *Proceedings of the 1991 Winter Simulation Conference*, 1991.

[21] Brandon Bloom, Christopher J. Dugan, Tedd Gimber, Bernard Goren, Andrew Hight, Moshe Kam, Joseph B. Kopena, Robert N. Lass, Israel Mayk, Spiros Mancoridis, Pragnesh Jay Modi, William M. Mongan, William C. Regli, Randy Reitmeyer, Jeff K. Salvage, Evan A. Sultanik, and Todd Urness. Agent Systems Reference Model. Technical report, US Army Communications and Electronics Command Research Development and Engineering Center (CERDEC), http://www.fipa.org/docs/ACIN-reference_model-v1a.pdf, November 2006. Release Version 1.0a.

[22] Eric Bonabeau. Agent-based modeling: Methods and techniques for simulating human systems. *Proceedings of the National Academy of Sciences of the United States of America*, 99(3):7280–7287, May 2002. 10.1073/pnas.082080899.

[23] Andrei Borshchev and Alexei Filippov. From System Dynamics and Discrete Event to Practical Agent Based Modeling: Reasons, Techniques, Tools. In *The 22nd International Conference of the Systems Dynamics Society*, Oxford, England, July 2004.

[24] Lars Braubach, Alexander Pokahr, Winfried Lamersdorf, Karl-Heinz Krempels, and Peer-Oliver Woelk. A Generic Simulation Service for Distributed Multi-Agent Systems. In Robert Trappl, editor, *Cybernetics and Systems 2004*, pages 576–581, Vienna, 2004. Austrian Society for Cybernetic Studies. 3-85206-169-5.

[25] Thomas M. Cioppa, Thomas W. Lucas, and Susan M. Sanchez. Military applications of agent-based simulations. In R. G. Ingalls, M. D. Rosetti, J. S. Smith, and B. A. Peters, editors, *Proceedings of the 2004 Winter Simulation Conference*, pages 171–180, 2004.

[26] Andrew Crooks, Christian Castle, and Michael Batty. Key challenges in agent-based modelling for geo-spatial simulation. *Computers, Environment and Urban Systems*, 32(6):417–430, November 2008.

[27] Paul Davidsson. Multi Agent Based Simulation: Beyond Social Simulation. In Scott Moss and Paul Davidsson, editors, *Multi-Agent-Based Simulation*, volume 1979 of *Lecture Notes in Computer Science*, pages 97–107, Berlin, Heidelberg, 2000. Springer-Verlag. doi:10.1007/3-540-44561-7.

[28] Paul Davidsson, Lawrence Henesey, Linda Ramstedt, Johanna Törnquist, and Fredrik Wernstedt. An analysis of agent-based approaches to transport logistics. *Transportation Research Part C: Emerging Technologies*, 13(4):255–271, August 2005.

[29] Robson E. De Grande and Azzedine Boukerche. Dynamic balancing of communication and computation load for HLA-based simulations on large-scale distributed systems. *Journal of Parallel and Distributed Computing*, 71(1):40–52, January 2011.

[30] Wieke de Vries, Frank S. de Boer, Wiebe van der Hoek, and John-Jules Ch. Meyer. A Truly Concurrent Model for Interacting Agents. In Soe-Tsyr Yuan and Makoto Yokoo, editors, *Intelligent Agents: Specification, Modeling, and Application*, volume 2132 of *Lecture Notes in Computer Science*, pages 16–30, Berlin, Heidelberg, 2001. Springer-Verlag. Proceedings of the 4th Pacific Rim International Workshop on Multi-Agents, PRIMA 2001, Taipei, Taiwan, July 28–29, 2001.

[31] Max Domeika. *Software Development for Embedded Multi-Core Systems: A Practical Guide Using Embedded Intel Architecture*. Elsevier, 2008.

[32] Robert Elsässer, Burkhard Monien, and Stefan Schamberger. Load Balancing of Indivisible Unit Size Tokens in Dynamic and Heterogeneous Networks. In Susanne Albers and Tomasz Radzik, editors, *Proceedings of the 12th Annual European Symposium on Algorithms*, volume 3221 of *Lecture Notes in Computer Science*, pages 640–651. Springer-Verlag, 2004. ESA 2004, September 14-17, 2004.

[33] Jacques Ferber and Jean-Pierre Müller. Influences and Reaction : a Model of Situated Multiagent Systems. In *Proceedings of the 2nd International Conference on Multi-agent Systems*, pages 72–79. AAAI Press, 1996. ICMAS 1996.

[34] Peter Fettke and Peter Loos. Referenzmodellierungsforschung – Langfassung eines Aufsatzes. Technical report, Johannes Gutenberg-University Mainz, ISYM - Information Systems & Management, Mainz, July 2004. ISSN 1617-6332.

[35] Michael Fisher. Representing and Executing Agent-Based Systems. In Michael J. Wooldridge and Nicholas R. Jennings, editors, *Intelligent Agents*, volume 890 of *Lecture Notes in Computer Science*, pages 307–323, Berlin, Heidelberg, 1995. Springer-Verlag. Proceedings of the ECAI-94 Workshop on

Agent Theories, Architectures, and Languages, Amsterdam, The Netherlands, August 8-9, 1994.

[36] Richard M. Fujimoto. *Parallel and Distributed Simulation Systems*. John Wiles & Sons, Inc., 2000.

[37] Samuel H. Fuller and Lynette I. Millett. *The Future of Computing Performance: Game Over or Next Level?* The National Academies Press, 2011. http://www.nap.edu/openbook.php?record_id=12980.

[38] Michael R. Garey and David S. Johnson. *Computers and Intractability: A Guide to the Theory of NP-Completeness*. W. H. Freeman and Company, New York, 1979.

[39] Michael R. Genesereth and Nils J. Nilsson. *Logische Grundlagen der Künstlichen Intelligenz*. Vieweg, Braunschweig, 1989.

[40] Christian Gerstner. Erweiterung und Implementierung eines Modells zur Analyse von Fragestellungen zur Koordination verteilter Organisationsstrukturen. Bachelorarbeit, Universität der Bundeswehr München, December 2009.

[41] Christian Gerstner, Robert Siegfried, and Nane Kratzke. Collaboration in Network-Centric Warfare – Modeling Joint Fire Support Teams. In *Proceedings of the Second International Workshop on Collaborative Agents - REsearch and Development (CARE) 2010*. IEEE/WIC/ACM, 2010.

[42] Christian Gerstner, Robert Siegfried, and Nane Kratzke. Agent-Based Simulation of Joint Fire Support Teams – Collaboration in Network-Centric Warfare Scenarios. In Christian Guttmann, Frank Dignum, and Michael Georgeff, editors, *Collaborative Agents – Research and Development*, volume 6066 of *Lecture Notes in Computer Science*, pages 56–67, Toronto, Canada, April 2011. Springer-Verlag. CARE@IAT 2010.

[43] Daniele Gianni, Andrea D'Ambrogio, and Giuseppe Iazeolla. A layered architecture for the model-driven development of distributed simulators. In *Proceedings of the 1st international conference on Simulation tools and techniques for communications, networks and systems & workshops*, pages 1–9, Brussels, Belgium, 2008. ICST (Institute for Computer Sciences, Social-Informatics and Telecommunications Engineering).

[44] Daniele Gianni, Andrea D'Ambrogio, and Giuseppe Iazeolla. DisSimJADE: A Framework for the development of Agent-based Distributed Simulation Systems. In *Proceedings of the 2nd International Conference on Simulation Tools and Techniques*, pages 1–10, Brussels, Belgium, 2009. ICST (Institute for Computer Sciences, Social-Informatics and Telecommunications Engineering).

[45] Brian Goetz, Tim Peierls, Joshua Bloch, Joseph Bowbeer, David Holmes, and Doug Lea. *Java Concurrency in Practice*. Addison-Wesley Longman, 2006.

[46] Richard Goodwin. Formalizing Properties of Agents. *Journal of Logic and Computation*, 5(6):763–781, December 1995. doi:10.1093/logcom/5.6.763.

[47] James Gosling, Bill Joy, Guy Steele, and Gilad Bracha. *The Java Language Specification*. Addison-Wesley, 3 edition, 2005.

[48] Chris Greenough, Shawn Chin, David Worth, Simon Coakley, Mike Holcombe, and Mariam Kiran. An Approach to the Parallelisation of Agent-Based Applications. *ERCIM News*, (81):42–43, April 2010. European Research Consortium for Informatics and Mathematics.

[49] Steffen Großmann. *Entwurf und Bewertung kombinierbarer Fehlertoleranzmechanismen bezüglich Betriebsfehlern in verteilten Simulationen*. PhD thesis, Universität der Bundeswehr München, 2010.

[50] László Gulyás and Sándor Bartha. FABLES: A Functional Agent-Based Language for Multi-Agent Simulations, 2005. Talk at the Meeting of the Technical Group on Programming Multi-Agent Systems, Budapest, Hungary.

[51] Alexander Helleboogh, Tom Holvoet, Danny Weyns, and Yolande Berbers. Towards Time Management Adaptability in Multi-agent Systems. In Daniel Kudenko, Dimitar Kazakov, and Eduardo Alonso, editors, *Adaptive Agents and Multi-Agent Systems III*, volume 3394 of *Lecture Notes in Computer Science*, pages 88–105, Berlin, Heidelberg, 2005. Springer-Verlag. doi:10.1007/b106974.

[52] Alexander Helleboogh, Giuseppe Vizzari, Adelinde M. Uhrmacher, and Fabien Michel. Modeling dynamic environments in multi-agent simulation. *Autonomous Agents and Multi-Agent Systems*, 14(1):87–116, February 2007.

[53] S. G. Henderson, B. Biller, M. H. Hsieh, J. Shortle, J. D. Tew, and R. R. Barton, editors. *Proceedings of the 2007 Winter Simulation Conference*, 2007.

[54] Wolfgang Hesse, Günter Merbeth, and Rainer Frölich. *Software-Entwicklung – Vorgehensmodelle, Projektführung, Produktverwaltung*. Oldenbourg Verlag, München, Wien, 1992.

[55] High-End Computing Revitalization Task Force. *Federal Plan for High-End Computing*. Report of the High-End Computing Revitalization Task Force (HECRTF). National Coordination Office for Information Technology Research and Development, Arlington, VA, USA, May 2004. http://www.nitrd.gov/pubs/2004_hecrtf/20040702_hecrtf.pdf.

[56] Jan Himmelspach, Roland Ewald, Stefan Leye, and Adelinde M. Uhrmacher. Enhancing the Scalability of Simulations by Embracing Multiple Levels of Parallelization. In *Proceedings of the*

2010 International Workshop on High Performance Computational Systems Biology, pages 57–66, 2010. PDMC-HiBi 2010, 30 September–1 October 2010.

[57] Jan Himmelspach and Adelinde M. Uhrmacher. The JAMES II Framework for Modeling and Simulation. In *Proceedings of the 2009 International Workshop on High Performance Computational Systems Biology*, pages 101–102, October 2009.

[58] Xiaolin Hu, Alexandre Muzy, and Lewis Ntaimo. A hybrid agent-cellular space modeling approach for fire spread and suppression simulation. In Kuhl et al. [72], pages 248–255.

[59] Michael N. Huhns and Larry M. Stephens. *Multiagent Systems – A Modern Approach to Distributed Artificial Intelligence*, chapter Multiagent, pages 79–120. The MIT Press, 1999.

[60] Nicholas R. Jennings. On agent-based software engineering. *Artificial Intelligence*, 117(2):277–296, March 2000. doi:10.1016/S0004-3702(99)00107-1.

[61] Nicholas R. Jennings, Katia Sycara, and Michael J. Wooldridge. A Roadmap of Agent Research and Development. *Autonomous Agents and Multi-Agent Systems*, 1(1):7–38, March 1998.

[62] Jeffrey A. Joines and Stephen D. Roberts. Fundamentals of object-oriented simulation. In D. J. Medeiros, E. F. Watson, John S. Carson II, and M. S. Manivannan, editors, *Proceedings of the 1998 Winter Simulation Conference*, pages 141–149, 1998.

[63] Cliff Joslyn and Luis M. Rocha. Towards Semiotic Agent-Based Models of Socio-Technical Organizations. In Hessam S. Sarjoughian, editor, *Proc. AI and Simulation 2000*, pages 70–79, 2000.

[64] Kaj Juslin. Experiences and Challenges in Development of Sustainable Modelling and Simulation Tools. *Simulation News Europe*, 20(1):27–30, April 2010. MATHMOD 2009.

[65] George Karypis and Vipin Kumar. A fast and high quality mul-
     tilevel scheme for partitioning irregular graphs. *SIAM Journal
     on Scientific Computing*, 20(1):359–392, 1999.

[66] Youmin Ke and Shanli Hu. A Concurrent Agent Model Based
     on Twin-Subset Semantic. In Zhong-Zhi Shi and Ramakoti
     Sadananda, editors, *Agent Computing and Multi-Agent Systems*,
     volume 4088 of *Lecture Notes in Computer Science*, pages 490–
     495, Berlin, Heidelberg, 2006. Springer-Verlag. Proceedings of
     the 9th Pacific Rim International Workshop on Multi-Agents,
     PRIMA 2006, Guilin, China, August 7–8, 2006.

[67] Tobias Kiesling. *Approximate Time-Parallel Simulation*. PhD
     thesis, Universität der Bundeswehr München, Neubiberg, Ger-
     many, December 2005.

[68] Franziska Klügl. Multiagentensimulation. *Informatik-Spektrum*,
     29(6):412–415, December 2006.

[69] Franziska Klügl. Towards a Formal Framework for Multi-Agent
     Simulation Models. Technical report, Institute of Computer
     Science, University of Würzburg, April 2007.

[70] Franziska Klügl, Manuel Fehler, and Rainer Herrler. About
     the Role of the Environment in Multi-agent Simulations. In
     Weyns et al. [145], pages 127–149. First International Workshop,
     E4MAS 2004, New York, NY, July 19, 2004, Revised Selected
     Papers.

[71] Franziska Klügl, Christoph Oechslein, Frank Puppe, and Anna
     Dornhaus. Multi-Agent Modelling in Comparison to Standard
     Modelling. In Fernando J. Barros and Norbert Giambiasi, edit-
     ors, *AIS'2002 (Artificial Intelligence, Simulation and Planning
     in High Autonomy Systems)*, pages 105–110. SCS Publishing
     House, 2002.

[72] Michael E. Kuhl, Natalie M. Steiger, F. Brad Armstrong, and
     Jeffrey A. Joines, editors. *Proceedings of the 37th Winter Sim-*

ulation Conference, Orlando, FL, USA, December 4-7, 2005. ACM, December 2005.

[73] Christoph Laroque, Jan Himmelspach, Raghu Pasupathy, Oliver Rose, and Adelinde M. Uhrmacher, editors. *Proceedings of the 2012 Winter Simulation Conference*, 2012.

[74] Averill Law and W. David Kelton. *Simulation Modeling and Analysis*. McGraw-Hill, 2000.

[75] Michael Lees, Brian Logan, Rob Minson, Ton Oguara, and Georgios Theodoropoulos. Distributed Simulation of MAS. In Paul Davidsson, Brian Logan, and Keiki Takadama, editors, *Multi-Agent and Multi-Agent-Based Simulation*, volume 3415 of *Lecture Notes in Computer Science*, pages 25–36, Berlin, Heidelberg, 2005. Springer-Verlag. Joint Workshop MABS 2004, New York, NY, USA, July 19, 2004, Revised Selected Papers.

[76] Michael Lees, Brian Logan, Rob Minson, Ton Oguara, and Georgios Theodoropoulos. Modelling Environments for Distributed Simulation. In Weyns et al. [145], pages 150–167. First International Workshop, E4MAS 2004, New York, NY, July 19, 2004, Revised Selected Papers.

[77] Axel Lehmann, Johannes Lüthi, Clemens Berchtold, Dirk Brade, and Andreas Köster. Zukunftsfelder der Modellbildung und Simulation. Abschlussbericht SKZ 12 990 Y 019 U, ITIS Institut für Technik Intelligenter Systeme e.V., 2000. VS-NfD.

[78] Brian Logan and Georgios Theodoropoulos. The Distributed Simulation of Multiagent Systems. *Proceedings of the IEEE*, 89(2):174–185, February 2001.

[79] Qingqi Long, Jie Lin, and Zhixun Sun. Agent scheduling model for adaptive dynamic load balancing in agent-based distributed simulations. *Simulation Modelling Practice and Theory*, 19(4):1021–1034, April 2011.

[80] Michael Luck and Mark d'Inverno. A Conceptual Framework for Agent Definition and Development. *The Computer Journal*, 44(1):1–20, 2001.

[81] Michael Luck, Peter McBurney, Onn Shehory, and Steve Willmott, editors. *Agent Technology: Computing as Interaction – A Roadmap for Agent Based Computing*. AgentLink III, September 2005.

[82] Thorsten Ludewig, Jochem Häuser, Torsten Gollnick, Wuye Dai, and Hans-Georg Paap. A Java Based High Performance Solver for Hierarchical Parallel Computer Architectures. In *Proceedings of 43rd AIAA Aerospace Sciences Meeting and Exhibit*, 2005. 10-13 January 2005, AIAA 2005-1383.

[83] Charles M. Macal and Michael J. North. Tutorial on agent-based modeling and simulation. In Kuhl et al. [72], pages 2–15.

[84] Michael W. Macy and Robert Willer. From Factors to Actors: Computational Sociology and Agent-Based Modeling. *Annual Review of Sociology*, 28:143–166, August 2002. doi:10.1146/annurev.soc.28.110601.141117.

[85] Pattie Maes. The Agent Network Architecture (ANA). *ACM SIGART Bulletin*, 2(4):115–120, August 1991.

[86] Dawit Mengistu, Peter Tröger, Lars Lundberg, and Paul Davidsson. Scalability in Distributed Multi-Agent Based Simulations: The JADE Case. In *2008 Second International Conference on Future Generation Communication and Networking Symposia*, pages 93–99. IEEE Computer Society, 2008. December 13–15.

[87] B. Scott Michel and Hans Zima. Workshop: Bridging Multicore's Programmability Gap, November 2008. International Conference for High Performance Computing, Networking, Storage and Analysis 2008, Austin, TX, USA.

[88] Nelson Minar, Roger Burkhart, Chris Langton, and Manor Askenazi. The Swarm Simulation System: A Toolkit for Building Multi-agent Simulations, June 1996.

[89] Jean-Pierre Müller. Towards a Formal Semantics of Event-Based Multi-agent Simulations. In Nuno David and Jaime Simão Sichmann, editors, *MABS 2008*, volume 5269 of *Lecture Notes in Computer Science*, pages 110–126, Berlin, Heidelberg, 2009. Springer-Verlag. International Workshop, MABS 2008, Estoril, Portugal, May 12-13, 2008, Revised Selected Papers.

[90] Jörg P. Müller. Control Architectures for Autonomous and Interacting Agents: A Survey. In Lawrence Cavedon, Anand Rao, and Wayne Wobcke, editors, *Intelligent Agent Systems Theoretical and Practical Issues*, volume 1209 of *Lecture Notes in Computer Science*, pages 1–26, Berlin, Heidelberg, 1997. Springer-Verlag. Based on a workshop held at PRICAI '96 Cairns, Australia, August 26–30, 1996.

[91] Pragnesh Jay Modi, William C. Regli, and Israel Mayk. The Case for a Reference Model for Agent-Based Systems. In *Proceedings of the IEEE Workshop on Distributed Intelligent Systems: Collective Intelligence and Its Applications, 2006. DIS 2006*, pages 321–325. IEEE Computer Society, June 2006. 10.1109/DIS.2006.69.

[92] Glenford J. Myers. *The Art of Software Testing*. John Wiley & Sons, 1979.

[93] Michael J. North and Charles M. Macal. *Managing business complexity: Discovering Strategic Solutions with Agent-Based Modeling and Simulation*. Oxford University Press, New York, 2007.

[94] James Nutaro and Hessam S. Sarjoughian. Design of Distributed Simulation Environments: A Unified System-Thoeretic

and Logical Processes Approach. *Simulation*, 80(11):577–589, November 2004.

[95] James Odell, H. Van Dyke Parunak, Mitch Fleischer, and Sven Brueckner. Modeling Agents and Their Environment. In Fausto Giunchiglia, James Odell, and Gerhard Weiss, editors, *Agent-Oriented Software Engineering III*, volume 2585 of *Lecture Notes in Computer Science*, pages 16–31, Berlin, Heidelberg, 2003. Springer-Verlag. doi:10.1007/3-540-36540-0_2.

[96] Fabio Y. Okuyama, Rafael H. Bordini, and Carlos da Rocha Costa. ELMS: An Environment Description Language for Multi-agent Simulation. In Weyns et al. [145], pages 91–108. First International Workshop, E4MAS 2004, New York, NY, July 19, 2004, Revised Selected Papers.

[97] Jon Parker. A flexible, large-scale, distributed agent based epidemic model. In Henderson et al. [53], pages 1543–1547.

[98] Hazel R. Parry and Andrew J. Evans. A comparative analysis of parallel processing and super-individual methods for improving the computational performance of a large individual-based model. *Ecological Modelling*, 214(2–4):141–152, June 2008.

[99] H. Van Dyke Parunak. Go to the ant: Engineering principles from natural multi-agent systems. *Annals of Operations Research*, 75(1):69–101, 1997.

[100] H. Van Dyke Parunak, Sven Brueckner, John Sauter, and Robert S. Matthews. Distinguishing Environmental and Agent Dynamics: A Case Study in Abstraction and Alternate Modeling Technologies. In *Engineering Societies in the Agents World*, volume 1972 of *Lecture Notes in Computer Science*, pages 19–33, Berlin, Heidelberg, 2000. Springer-Verlag.

[101] Dirk Pawlaszczyk. *Skalierbare agentenbasierte Simulation : Werkzeuge und Techniken zur verteilten Ausführung agen-*

tenbasierter Modelle. PhD thesis, TU Ilmenau, May 2009. urn:nbn:de:gbv:ilm1-2009000177.

[102] Mauro Pezzè and Michal Young. *Software Testing and Analysis: Process, Principles, and Techniques.* John Wiley & Sons, 2008.

[103] Martha E. Pollack and Marc Ringuette. Introducing the Tileworld: Experimentally Evaluating Agent Architectures. In *Proceedings of the Eighth National Conference on Artificial Intelligence*, pages 183–189. AAAI, 1990.

[104] Bernd Preiss and Carey Ka Wing Wan. The Parsimony Project: A Distributed Simulation Testbed in Java. In *Proceedings of 1999 International Conference On Web-Based Modelling & Simulation*, volume 31 of *Simulation Series*, pages 89–94. Society for Computer Simulation, January 1999.

[105] President's Information Technology Advisory Committee. *Computational Science: Ensuring America's Competitiveness.* Report to the President. National Coordination Office for Information Technology Research and Development, Arlington, VA, USA, June 2005. http://www.nitrd.gov/Pitac/reports/20050609_computational/computational.pdf.

[106] Markus Rabe, Sven Spieckermann, and Sigrid Wenzel. *Verifikation und Validierung für die Simulation in Produktion und Logistik: Vorgehensmodelle und Techniken.* Springer-Verlag, Berlin, 2008.

[107] Wolf-Ulrich Raffel. *Agentenbasierte Simulation als Verfeinerung der Diskreten-Ereignis-Simulation unter besonderer Berücksichtigung des Beispiels Fahrerloser Transportsysteme.* PhD thesis, Freie Universität Berlin, March 2005.

[108] William C. Regli, Israel Mayk, Christopher J. Dugan, Joseph B. Kopena, Robert N. Lass, Pragnesh Jay Modi, William M. Mongan, Jeff K. Salvage, and Evan A. Sultanik. Development and

Specification of a Reference Model for Agent-Based Systems. *IEEE Transactions on Systems, Man, and Cybernetics, Part C: Applications and Reviews*, 39(5):572–596, September 2009.

[109] Patrick Riley. MPADES: Middleware for Parallel Agent Discrete Event Simulation. In Gal A. Kaminka, Pedro U. Lima, and Paul Rojas, editors, *RoboCup 2002: Robot Soccer World Cup VI*, volume 2752 of *Lecture Notes in Computer Science*, pages 162–178, Berlin, Heidelberg, 2003. Springer-Verlag.

[110] Patrick Riley and George Riley. SPADES – A Distributed Agent Simulation Environment with Software-in-the-loop execution. In S. Chick, P. J. Sánchez, D. Ferrin, and D. J. Morrice, editors, *Proceedings of the 2003 Winter Simulation Conference*, pages 817–825, 2003.

[111] Ralph Rogers and Gary Harless. Improving Computational Efficiency in Autonomous Agent, Asynchronous Discrete-Event Simulation. *Systems, Man, and Cybernetics, 1994. 'Humans, Information and Technology'., 1994 IEEE International Conference on*, 1:227–232, 1994. doi:10.1109/ICSMC.1994.399841.

[112] Stuart J. Russell and Peter Norvig. *Artificial Intelligence – A Modern Approach*. Pearson Education, Inc., 2 edition, 2003.

[113] Nicole J. Saam. Simulating the Micro-Macro Link: New Approaches to an Old Problem and an Application to Military Coups. *Sociological Methodology*, 29(1):43–79, 1999.

[114] Matthias Scheutz and Paul Schermerhorn. Adaptive algorithms for the dynamic distribution and parallel execution of agent-based models. *Journal of Parallel and Distributed Computing*, 66(8):1037–1051, August 2006.

[115] Bernd Schmidt and Bernhard Schneider. Agent- based Modelling of Human Acting, Deciding and Behaviour - The Reference Model PECS. In Graham Horton, editor, *Network Simulations*

and Simulated Networks, pages 378–387. SCS Europe, 2004. Proceedings of the 18th European Simulation Multiconference 2004.

[116] Michael Schumacher and Sascha Ossowski. The Governing Environment. In Danny Weyns, H. Van Dyke Parunak, and Fabien Michel, editors, *Environments for Multi-Agent Systems II*, volume 3830 of *Lecture Notes in Computer Science*, pages 88–104, Berlin, Heidelberg, 2006. Springer-Verlag.

[117] Aamir Shafi, Bryan Carpenter, and Mark Baker. Nested parallelism for multi-core HPC systems using Java. *Journal of Parallel and Distributed Computing*, 69(6):532–545, June 2009.

[118] Ruchir Shah, Bhardwaj Veeravalli, and Manoj Misra. On the Design of Adaptive and Decentralized Load-Balancing Algorithms with Load Estimation for Computational Grid Environments. *IEEE Transactions on Parallel and Distributed Systems*, 18(12):1675–1686, December 2007.

[119] Jim Shore. Fail Fast. *IEEE Software*, 21(5):21–25, 2004.

[120] Peer-Olaf Siebers and Uwe Aickelin. Introduction to Multi-Agent Simulation. Preprint for encyclopedia of decision making and decision support technologies, University of Nottingham, 2007. http://eprints.nottingham.ac.uk/645/.

[121] Robert Siegfried and Axel Lehmann. Application of the GRAMS Reference Model for Agent-Based Modeling and Simulation to a Warehouse Scenario. In *Proceedings of the Spring Simulation Multiconference*. SCS, April 2010. Agent-Directed Simulation Symposium.

[122] SISO. Fidelity Implementation Study Group Report. SISO Reference Product SISO-REF-002-1999, Simulation Interoperability Standards Organization (SISO), Orlando, FL, USA, 1999.

[123] Aaron Sloman. What sort of architecture is required for a human-like agent? In Michael J. Wooldridge and Anand Rao, editors, *Foundations of Rational Agency*, Applied Logic Series, pages 35–52. Kluwer Academic Publishers, 1999.

[124] Alexander Steiniger, Frank Krüger, and Adelinde M. Uhrmacher. Modeling agents and their environment in ml-DEVS. In Laroque et al. [73].

[125] Jeffrey S. Steinman. Introduction to Parallel and Distributed Force Modeling and Simulation. In *Proceedings of 2009 Spring Simulation Interoperability Workshop (SIW)*. Simulation Interoperability Standards Organization (SISO), The Society for Modeling and Simulation International (SCS), March 2009. 09S-SIW-021.

[126] Xian-He Sun and Yong Chen. Reevaluating Amdahl's law in the multicore era. *Journal of Parallel and Distributed Computing*, 70(2):183–188, February 2010.

[127] Georgios Theodoropoulos and Brian Logan. A Framework for the Distributed Simulation of Agent-based Systems. In Helena Szczerbicka, editor, *Modelling and Simulation: a tool for the next millennium, Proceedings of the 13th European Simulation Multiconference (ESM 99)*, volume 1, pages 58–65. SCS, Society for Computer Simulation International, Society for Computer Simulation International, June 1999.

[128] Georgios Theodoropoulos and Brian Logan. An Approach to Interest Management and Dynamic Load Balancing in Distributed Simulation. In *Proceedings of the 2001 European Simulation Interoperability Workshop (ESIW 01)*, pages 565–571. SISO/SCS, June 2001.

[129] Oliver Thomas. Das Referenzmodellverständnis in der Wirtschaftsinformatik: Historie, Literaturanalyse und Begriffsexplikation. Technical Report 187, Deutsches Forschungszen-

trum für Künstliche Intelligenz, Institut für Wirtschaftsinformatik, Saarbrücken, January 2006. ISSN 1438 5678.

[130] Oliver Thomas. Understanding the Term Reference Model in Information Systems Research: History, Literature Analysis and Explanation. In Christoph Bussler and Armin Haller, editors, *Business Process Management Workshops*, volume 3812 of *Lecture Notes in Computer Science*, pages 484–496, Berlin, Heidelberg, 2006. Springer-Verlag.

[131] Adelinde M. Uhrmacher. Dynamic Structures in Modeling and Simulation: A Reflective Approach. *ACM Transactions on Modeling and Computer Simulation*, 11(2):206–232, April 2001.

[132] Adelinde M. Uhrmacher and R. Arnold. Distributing and Maintaining Knowledge: Agents in Variable Structure Environments. In *Proceedings of the Fifth Annual Conference on AI, Simulation, and Planning in High Autonomy Systems*, pages 178–184. IEEE Computer Society Press, December 1994.

[133] Adelinde M. Uhrmacher, Roland Ewald, Mathias John, Carsten Maus, Matthias Jeschke, and Susanne Biermann. Combining micro and macro-modeling in DEVS for computational biology. In Henderson et al. [53], pages 871–880.

[134] Adelinde M. Uhrmacher and K. Gugler. Distributed, Parallel Simulation of Multiple, Deliberative Agents. In *PADS '00: Proceedings of the fourteenth workshop on Parallel and distributed simulation*, pages 101–108, Washington, DC, USA, 2000. IEEE Computer Society.

[135] Christoph Urban. *Das Referenzmodell PECS – Agentenbasierte Modellierung menschlichen Handelns, Entscheidens und Verhaltens*. PhD thesis, Universität Passau, April 2004.

[136] Gerd Wagner. The Agent-Object-Relationship metamodel: towards a unified view of state and behavior. *Information Systems*, 28(5):475–504, July 2003.

[137] Gerd Wagner. AOR Modelling and Simulation: Towards a General Architecture for Agent-Based Discrete Event Simulation. In Paolo Giorgini, Brian Henderson-Sellers, and Michael Winikoff, editors, *Agent-Oriented Simulation Systems*, volume 3030/2004 of *Lecture Notes in Computer Science*, pages 174–188, Berlin, Heidelberg, 2004. Springer-Verlag. 5th International Bi-Conference Workshop, AOIS 2003, Melbourne, Australia, July 14, 2003 and Chicago, IL, USA, October 13th, 2003, Revised Selected Papers.

[138] Gerd Wagner, Adrian Giurca, Marco Pehla, and Jens Werner. Modellierung und Simulation von Multiagenten-Systemen. *Forum der Forschung*, 21:47–52, 2008. BTU Cottbus, Eigenverlag.

[139] Gerd Wagner and Florin Tulba. Agent-Oriented Modeling and Agent-Based Simulation. In Manfred A. Jeusfeld and Óscar Pastor, editors, *Proceedings of ER 2003 Workshops*, volume 2814 of *Lecture Notes in Computer Science*, pages 205–216, Berlin, Heidelberg, 2003. Springer-Verlag.

[140] Gabriel A. Wainer. *Discrete-event modeling and simulation: a practitioner's approach*. CRC Press, 2009.

[141] Gerhard Weiss, editor. *Multiagent Systems – A Modern Approach to Distributed Artificial Intelligence*. The MIT Press, 1999.

[142] Daniel Weyel. Erweiterung und Implementierung eines Modells zur Analyse von Fragestellungen zur Koordination verteilter Organisationsstrukturen bei der Feuerwehr. Bachelorarbeit, Universität der Bundeswehr München, December 2010.

[143] Danny Weyns and Tom Holvoet. Model for Situated Multi-Agent Systems with Regional Synchronization. In *10th International Conference on Concurrent Engineering, Agent and Multi-Agent Systems*. Balkema Publishers, July 2003. CE'03.

[144] Danny Weyns and Tom Holvoet. A Formal Model for Situated Multi-Agent Systems. *Fundamenta Informaticae*, 63:1–34, 2004.

[145] Danny Weyns, H. Van Dyke Parunak, and Fabien Michel, editors. *Environments for Multi-Agent Systems*, volume 3374 of *Lecture Notes in Computer Science*, Berlin, Heidelberg, 2005. Springer-Verlag. First International Workshop, E4MAS 2004, New York, NY, July 19, 2004, Revised Selected Papers.

[146] Danny Weyns, H. Van Dyke Parunak, Fabien Michel, Tom Holvoet, and Jacques Ferber. Environments for Multiagent Systems State-of-the-Art and Research Challenges. In Weyns et al. [145], pages 1–47. First International Workshop, E4MAS 2004, New York, NY, July 19, 2004, Revised Selected Papers.

[147] Danny Weyns, Elke Steegmans, and Tom Holvoet. Towards Active Perception in Situated Multi-Agent Systems. *Applied Artificial Intelligence*, 18(9 & 10):867–883, October 2004. doi:10.1080/08839510490509063.

[148] Michael J. Wooldridge. *Intelligent Agents*, chapter 1, pages 27–77. In Weiss [141], 1999.

[149] Michael J. Wooldridge. *An Introduction to Multi-Agent Systems*. Wiley & Sons, 1 edition, 2002.

[150] Michael J. Wooldridge. *An Introduction to MultiAgent Systems*. John Wiley & Sons, 2 edition, 2009.

[151] Bernard P. Zeigler, Herbert Praehofer, and Tag Gon Kim. *Theory of Modeling and Simulation – Integrating Discrete Event and Continuous Complex Dynamic Systems*. Academic Press, San Diego, 2 edition, 2000.

The manufacturer's authorised representative in the EU is Springer
Nature Customer Service Centre GmbH, Europaplatz 3, 69115 Heidelberg,
Germany. If you have any concerns regarding our products, please
contact ProductSafety@springernature.com

Printed and bound by CPI Group (UK) Ltd, Croydon, CR0 4YY
27/04/2026
02097645-0001